# TRUST YOUR MOTHER BUT CUT THE CARDS

Sidney Zion

Barricade Books Inc.
Fort Lee, New Jersey

Published by Barricade Books Inc.
1530 Palisade Avenue
Fort Lee, NJ 07024

Distributed by Publishers Group West
4065 Hollis
Emeryville, CA 94608

Printed in the United States of America.

Library of Congress Cataloging-in-Publication Data

Zion, Sidney.
    Trust your mother but cut the cards / Sidney Zion.
    ISBN: 0-942637-77-1
    1. Title.
PS3576.I556L68   1993                    92-35526
                                         CIP


0 9 8 7 6 5 4 3 2 1

For Adam and Jed, my sparkling
boys, in order of their appearance.

❏❏❏

And to Johnnie Walker,
without whom none of this
would have happened.

## Also by Sidney Zion

*Read All About It! The Collected Adventures of a Maverick Reporter*

*The Autobiography of Roy Cohn*

*Markers*

# CONTENTS

v

# Author's Note

W hen asked what comes first, the words or the music, Sammy Cahn said, "The phone call." This book was made by two phone calls, if you want to look at it that way.

In the late spring of 1991, Arthur Carter, the publisher of the weekly *New York Observer*, called to ask if I was interested in resuming my column in the paper. I liked the way he put it, "resuming." I hadn't written for *The Observer* for four years, or since its first two issues.

My leave taking had nothing to do with Arthur or the paper; I was backed up with two books. Now I had only one book on the menu and was ready. It didn't hurt that in the meantime *The Observer* had become a hot paper, something like *The Village Voice* was in the 1960's: "Everybody" was reading it, forget about circulation numbers.

Six months later, Lyle Stuart called.

"Those columns you've been writing in *The Observer* ought to be a book," he said. "Everybody's talking about them. Are you interested?"

No more than I was at 14 when my Cousin Willy asked me whether I wanted to go to the Stadium to see the Yankees play the Dodgers in the '47 World Series.

1

But were there enough columns to make a book?

"We're not putting it out until next year," Lyle said.

"You know," I said, "I've got plenty of other stuff."

It had been ten years since my first collection *Read All About It!* was published. In the interim I had written a gang of pieces, printed everywhere from *The New York Times* to *The Nation* to *National Review* to *Penthouse.*

"Get 'em over to me," said Lyle.

Most of them appear here.

Then, running through my mother's archive, I discovered a file labeled "Roots." It turned out to contain a bunch of pieces about my home town, Passaic. Published more than fifteen years ago in the New Jersey section of *The New York Times.*

I had forgotten all about them. And here they were in momma's trunk, hidden beneath my Uncle Chick's bar mitzvah pictures.

Trust your mother but cut the cards.

# I

## THE JEWISH MAFIA

# KOSHER NOSTRA COCKTAIL

Let's see what kind of cocktail I can shake out of these ingredients: Gay Talese, John Gotti, Roy Cohn, Lepke Buchalter, Longy Zwillman, Bill Clinton, the Beatles, Artie Shaw, Cole Porter, Jerry Brown, Jesse Jackson, George Bush, Sophie Tucker and the Biltmore clock.

Gay Talese, my main man, my buddy, my mentor, writes the morning-after kaddish for John Gotti on the Op-Ed page of *The Times*, and there I am in my bed nodding and smiling Gay Talese home, when suddenly the following line jumps out of the paper and into my face:

"Will the Mafia's dominant status in the underworld, earned during the Prohibition era by outwitting and outshooting the Jewish and Irish gangs . . ."

Well, I will let Pete Hamill speak for his people, or Captain Sam, who guards the rope at Gallagher's, or Paul O'Dwyer or the Great Boniface James Clare of County Dublin. It falls to me to defend the honor of my Jews, things being how they are these days at the Anti-Defamation League. I pledge that I will not

5

fail the ghost of Israel Schawarzberg, who long ago taught me the mantra: "Time was the Jews was everything."

Come with me now to the East Side town house of Roy M. Cohn, Esq., where the host is throwing himself a birthday party. The year is 1975, or a couple of deals before these parties metasticized to Studio 54 and became the hottest show in town.

I recognize a face in the crowd as being that of a former hit man for Mr. Lepke Buchalter. I ask Mr. Cohn to provide the introduction, as I am embarked on a study of the Jewish mobs that I feel may turn out to be a book. Roy takes my arm and does the job as follows: "He's doing a book on the Jewish Mafia. He's a friend, you can talk to him."

The gentleman talks to me: "What are you doing *that* for?" he says.

I don't like his eyes right now. I say, "For the money."

He nods. "It could be a good score, kid. What are you finding out?"

"Well," I say, "I'm finding out that the Jews were more important than people think."

"More important than who?"

"Just more important than people think."

"Than *who*," he says, his finger in my chest.

"Well," I say, "not as big as the Italians, but more important than . . ."

Now the finger is like a .38, I can't even get the next word out.

"You think we took orders from *guineas*?"

Immediately, the mantra comes back to me. Israel Shawarzberg died with his shoes off five years before, but his mantra now plays in my head like an under-world knockoff of the Kol Nidre.

Timewasthejewswaseverythingtimewasthejews waseverything . . .

And to think I never believed him! Izzy, the last great single-act in an American underworld gone soft with corporate-style bureaucracy. Just because he never qualified for the Mount Rushmore of crime, I dished his mantra off in favor of what? Joe Valachi and Peter Maas! Mr. Israel, who only pioneered the college basketball fix! Who in his spare time fixed horses, cops and witnesses, who swindled banks and shylocks and Mafia dons. And I didn't believe him.

*You think we took orders from guineas?*

I went straight to work, and though I still haven't written the book, I wish you could tap into my files. It's a tossup whether the Mafia mavens or the B'nai B'rith will be more embarrassed by the names that dominated the rackets from the 20's through the mid-50's, but facts are facts and let the vowels fall where they may.

So: Arnold Rothstein, Moses Annenberg, Dutch Goldberg, Waxey Gordon, Meyer Lansky, Bugsy Siegel, Longy Zwillman, Doc Stacher, Dutch Schultz, Lepke Buchalter, Gurrah Shapiro, Moe Dalitz, Nig Rosen, Boo Hoff, Isador (Kid Cann) Blumenfield, Toot-sie Herbert—not to mention the Detroit Purple Gang and Murder Inc.

Outwitted and outshot by the Mafia?

Let me tell you something, Mr. Gay Talese. When your ancestors were walking on grapes in cold-water Mulberry Street bathtubs, mine were wetting America's whistles with Mr. Johnnie Walker Black. Longy

Zwillman all by himself brought in half the hootch from Canada, and who do you think bottled the stuff up there, or did you never hear of Bronfmans?

Nor was it just booze, of course not. Who invented Las Vegas, baby, who but Mr. Benjamin Siegel? Who invented the Teamsters, who but Mr. Lepke and Mr. Gurrah and Mr. Goldberg?

Sure it ended, we put the date circa 1956. But not because your guys outwitted and outgunned us.

Back to Roy Cohn's town house that black-tie night in 1975.

I say this to the former Lepke *shtarker*, now a prosperous Manhattan businessman, I say: "But how come all I see when I look around are Italians?"

He says: "What did you do when you decided to be 18 years old?"

"I went to college," I say.

"So?"

"So what?" I say.

"We lost our farm system."

Thus was the end of the Jewish Empire. The children were turned over to the mothers and ended up in Harvard and Yale and even West Point. John Gotti Jr. lives (for now) but we never had any Lepke Jr. L'chaim!

I promised a bigger cocktail, but space is a jigger so I had better shake fast.

I read in the papers that Bill Clinton can't find a campaign song. His legions run through the rock canon and if the lyrics don't O.D., the composers have.

Kurt Vonnegut wrote: "True terror is to wake up one morning and discover that your high school class is running the country."

How much worse to wake up and discover that the Woodstock generation is running the Democratic Party?

Gertrude Stein didn't know what she was talking about. The real Lost Generation is mine, the guys and dolls born in the early 30's. We were labeled The Silent Generation, and it looks now that we will be silent to the end. For us, they're either too young or too old.

George Bush is the Second World War. Bill Clinton and Jerry Brown are Vietnam. Where is Korea?

We were good kids, we really were, I swear it. We were the last to know Artie Shaw, the first to read J.D. Salinger. We brought back Hemingway and Faulkner, and we actually met the blind dates under the clock at the Biltmore.

If we were lucky enough to go to college, we didn't have to go to Korea, but our less fortunate brothers went and fought valiantly. We took no hard drugs, we knew no hard porn and our parents didn't even get divorced. We were good kids, we really were, I swear it.

But unless there's a late bloomer out there, we are not going to make it to the top.

And Bill Clinton can't find a campaign song. If he was one of us, he'd have a million of 'em. How about *Makin' Whoopie*? If he knew Cole Porter, would he not be singing *Let's Do It*?

On the other hand, he has the perfect song without us Tommy Dorsey freaks. The Beatles. *Why Don't We Do It in the Road*?

Don't get me wrong. I hate George Bush.

Here comes Sophie Tucker with the theme song for the Democrats.

*Never Let the Same Dog Bite You Twice.*

And there is my cocktail. Everything in it but Jesse Jackson.

No good Jewish bartender would slip you a mickey.

# FIXING LITTLE MENDEL

This happened in the reign of Dopey Benny Fein, circa 1912, the Lower East Side.

One of Benny's lads, remembered only as Little Mendel, was caught holding up a poolroom on Second Avenue. Promptly removed to the nearest squeal room, Little Mendel was reminded by detectives that he was now about to become a four-time loser. This of course meant a whole life in *durance vile*, unless . . .

All Little Mendel had to do to avoid this terrible fate was to tell the detectives the whereabouts of a certain party with whom they were eager to meet. As this party was a friend and compatriot and a member in good standing of the Dopey Benny Fein organization, Little Mendel was of course loath to disclose his whereabouts. "I don't know nothin," Little Mendel said.

Various persuasive methods were employed to jog his memory, but to no avail. And then a nice Irish detective appeared on the scene and said: "Who will know, Mendel, tell me who will know? Give us the whereabouts of this fellow and you can leave now. And who will know? You think we'll give you the credit?"

Ordinarily, a wise lad like Little Mendel would be suspicious of this logic, but as he thought more about

11

life in *durance vile* he began to recall several slights inflicted upon him by this so-called friend the police wanted to meet, and soon enough he decided that the nice Irish detective was absolutely right and now he remembered just where the bastard was hiding out on the Jersey Shore.

Well, things being how they were in those days on the Lower East Side, Dopey Benny's headquarters received the news of Little Mendel's memory even before the coppers could draw the necessary vouchers for the trip to Bradley Beach.

And so, no sooner was Little Mendel breathing the beautiful air of freedom than he was taken on a walk to a doctor's home in the neighborhood. It happened that this doctor was a dear friend of Dopey Benny's and furthermore was Dopey Benny's doctor, which meant that he was the doctor for all needs of Dopey Benny's people, such as gunshot wounds and this and that.

Since there was nothing wrong with Little Mendel's health, there was no need to take his medical history or even examine him. The doctor simply had to follow the instructions of Dopey Benny Fein.

The instructions were simple: Cut his spinal cord.

And it was done and Little Mendel was rendered a quadraplegic.

But that is not the end of this story, it is practically only the beginning.

For it was not Dopey Benny's intention to merely seek retribution; if that's all he was after he'd have had Little Mendel rubbed out, in the style of the city's Italian mob.

No. The purpose was deterrence. Little Mendel

was the first rat and Dopey Benny was determined that
he would be the last.

He was set up in an apartment and provided with
around-the-clock nursing care. Not for comfort, but to
keep him alive—and keep him from committing
suicide.

The Jewish mobs did not induct youths with cere-
mony, nor was there an oath of *omerta.*

But nobody got into Dopey Benny's outfit without
a visit to Little Mendel.

The established ritual was a party: drinks and food
and music at Little Mendel's bedside. Everybody having a good time, the hoods and their girls and, of
course, the new hopeful.

Little Mendel lived for many years in this manner,
long after Dopey Benny Fein had left the scene. Dopey
Benny died broke, but his disciples included Waxey
Gordon, Lepke Buchalter, Gurrah Shapiro and Dutch
Goldberg, all of whom waxed rich and powerful during
and after Prohibition.

Did they all visit Little Mendel in his bed as
initiation?

Who will know, Mendel, who will know?

What we do know is that no Jewish mobster ratted
again until Abe Reles gave up Lepke in 1940. And look
what happened to Abe Reles.

Without a Witness Protection Act, Abe Reles had
what no mafiosi has had since: nine police officers
guarding his sleep at the Half Moon Hotel in Coney
Island. And yet, he ended his days in the very court-
yard of that hotel, a canary who could sing but couldn't
fly.

The next Jew who ratted out a Jew was David Greenglass, Julius Rosenberg's brother-in-law. But what did those Commies know about Little Mendel?

Well, the story I have just told is a story never before writ, so how could David Greenglass know? How could Salvatore Gravano know? How could John Gotti know?

The history of the Jewish mobs is practically non-existent, despite what you may think you learned in the movie *Bugsy*. There are many reasons for this, including the very good idea that the subjects had, to wit: Who needs publicity? Nor has the Anti-Defamation League been interested in pursuing the deal.

I think differently. I think we Jews need to know that we had *shtarkers*, that we are not just accountants to the Mafia, that time was when the Jews ran organized crime in America. And that the Jewish mobsters decided not to keep going. They turned their sons over to the mothers and saw them become lawyers and doctors and whatever.

Anyway, Little Mendel came back to mind when I ran over to Brooklyn to see Sammy the Bull give his best on the witness stand against his old boss, John Gotti.

I understood then and there what had gone wrong with the old Unione Sicilione.

It was not, I hasten to say, a matter of spinal cords. Just good old bureaucracy.

John Gotti walks into the courtroom and immediately all eyes turn. He radiates charisma, he is the show, of course, you all know that. It doesn't matter that his bespoke suit radiates the Republic of Queens by the matching tie and handkerchief, he is the show.

And there is Sammy the Bull, bespoke as well, and even better for the difference in tie and hanky.

But two words out of his mouth tell all. Salvatore Gravano is a sub-editor.

John Gotti understood what every editor in chief understands, what every legitimate boss in business for that matter understands: Never put a guy stronger than me under me. Paul Castellano pushes up daisies now because he forgot or never knew that rule. He was, after all, a man promoted through nepotism, he was Carlo Gambino's brother-in-law, he was *mishpucha*.

But nepotism, as the Jewish gangsters knew, is a recipe for disaster, for it is bottomed on vanity, and vanity kills its own children.

Castellano could know nothing of this, by definition. He made John Gotti a capo without fear. What can he do to me?

John Gotti, vanity bespoke, would nonetheless never make that mistake.

Salvatore Gravano was the perfect underling, a goodfella looking only to take orders.

Sammy the Bull would never dream to kill John Gotti.

What can he do to me?

Nothing, if a sub-editor, if in any legit game.

In the mob, a guy who can't kill you has only one alternative.

Who will know, Little Mendel, who will know?

# BUGSY & MEYER

Faye Emerson opened in a Broadway turkey once and Walter Kerr closed it with a one-line review: "They shouldn't have done it to Fayzie."

That had to be 35 years ago, yet it didn't take but 35 minutes into *Bugsy* for it to jump right out of my subconscious mind and into the ear of my ever-loving wife. "They shouldn't have done it to Benny," I said, or let me say I hissed, because I get very hot when Hollywood does wrong by my great Jewish gangsters.

Of course, Hollywood has never done right by them, not that it ever did much about them. In the halcyon days of the big studios, when the Jews ran the show, you'd never have known that the Jews ran the underworld. Indeed, you'd never know they were part of it—in movies of the 30's, 40's and 50's, they weren't even accountants to the mob.

Jews like Paul Muni, Edward G. Robinson and Luther Adler were allowed to play mobsters but they were always Italians. As far as I know, the Anti-Defamation League never lodged a complaint against this disappearance of the Jewish gangster. And probably Mr. Benjamin Siegel would have lodged something else up their something elses if Mr. Goldwyn or Mr. Mayer

**17**

or Mr. Cohn decided to do biographies of Mr. Lansky, Mr. Lepke, Mr. Zwillman or Mr. Dalitz.

This was very disturbing to us Jewish kids growing up in the 40's, at least us Passaic guys. Gangsters are the most powerful role models ever conjured up in film, and it galled us that they turned John Garfield into a goy, and Edward G. and the rest of those marvelous *shtarkers*. We knew the Jews of Europe were getting slaughtered, but here there were no Jews playing Jews in the movies. This wasn't just gangsters, you couldn't even play a Jewish businessman, much less a lover, during the Second World War.

When Jews finally started appearing as Jews on screen, they all played one form or other of Woody Allen's neurotic nebbish. No mobsters — forget about it.

In *The Godfather*, Bugsy Siegel is Moe Green, portrayed as a loudmouth Jew who owes everything to the Mafia. He's whacked out on a massage table because he won't sell the casino to Don Corleone. The Jews ran Vegas in those days, so this was pure fantasy, but it seemed real to most people because Mafia hegemony is assumed, and is assumed to have been the case back then, when it surely did not exist.

A Lansky character named Hyman Roth is shown more respect in *Godfather, Part II*, but in the end the Italians have him murdered at the airport after he's kicked out of Israel. This outraged Meyer, don't you think it didn't, and I didn't like it either, nor did my old pals from the hometown. I mean, here Meyer outlives all those bums without doing more than three months in the slammer his entire long life, and they bump him off like he's nothing but a politician.

The first *Godfather* movies were received with

contempt by the old Jewish sluggers who used to congregate for kugel and schnapps at the late great Mendel's Bar & Grill on Clinton Street. I asked Red Levine,
of sainted memory, what he thought of them knocking
off Lansky. Red had been one of Meyer's top guns and
he spat on the floor of Mendel's Bar & Grill when I
asked him about the movie. He said, "It never happened. Fuhgetaboutit!" Then he said: "Them bastards!
I don't know why we let 'em get away with that
bullshit."

I try now to imagine what Red Levine would have
said if he had lived to see *Bugsy*. Because of course if
you worked for Lansky you worked for Siegel. It all
began as the Bug and Meyer gang, pronounced Bug-
a-Meyer. Oh, and look how Warren Beatty & Co. have
massacred Benjamin Siegel, not to mention the truth.

Fictionalization is what movies are about, I'm hip,
but it's supposed to make the story better, no? Here
they turn diamonds into rhinestones.

Warren Beatty's Siegel starts out with promise: the
swagger, the jolt, he even looks a little like the Bug. But
soon he goes to Hollywood and everything changes,
which may be a metaphor for our time, but not necessarily for that time. The picture is set entirely in the
40's, which is fine, although Siegel went out there in
1935. Sequence switches are O.K., but it's not so O.K.
that he goes to Hollywood to take over the rackets.
That was practically a side issue. The idea was to get
the grab on the movie studios.

This Ben Siegel did brilliantly. He was out of central casting, and he charmed the moguls even as he was
fleecing them. In quick time, he organized the extras,
which nobody had thought to do. The big Hollywood

movies, especially the musicals, needed extras like they needed film. Threaten a strike during a production and what do you have?

It came out of the garment center textbook as written by Lepke Buchalter and a little-known but powerhouse figure named Louis Shomberg, also known as Papa Louie (a sobriquet given him by Ben Siegel) and as Dutch Goldberg. Lepke and Papa Louie noticed in the Roaring Twenties that nobody had organized the truck drivers. There were 50 truck drivers. If you owned them, nobody could ship without you. They owned the garment center, forget about the legit unions.

Warren Beatty's Siegel is interested only in deposing the Italian, Jack Dragna, which takes two minutes. And then all he can think about is Virginia Hill, who dominates his every move.

The movie makes him a slave to Virginia Hill, and there's a better word for it, as in youthful cats and you know the rest. There is something to this history. Like a lot of other mobsters, he went bonkers over Miss Hill, who turned out to be the most famous sex witness in a Senate hearing until Anita Hill, no relation. When the Senate organized crime investigation headed by Estes Kefauver met in executive session in 1951, Miss Hill was asked why so many mobsters were in her thrall. She said: "Because Senator, I am the best cocksucker in the world."

Nonetheless, Virginia Hill was not the proximate cause of Bugsy Siegel's demise, as the film would have it. The real story is better and richer and maybe they didn't know it, but I know it, and now you'll know it.

Siegel invented Las Vegas, that's so, and the movie

says so and says so until you get bored silly. He built the Flamingo at an enormous cost overrun, which upset his partners, particularly Lucky Luciano. What gets him killed in the flick is that they discover Virginia Hill has deposited $2 million in Switzerland. Lansky, his best friend, sadly orders the hit. And the Flamingo, losing a fortune, is saved.

But the Flamingo was actually turning a big profit by the time Siegel was hit in 1947. When the Mob found out about the skimming and the secret bank account, they wanted to meet with Siegel, mainly to let him know they knew—and maybe get the dough back into the kitty.

Siegel thought it was a sitdown, as in a death sentence. He told Papa Louie, then the top boss, to call off the meet. But Papa Louie had shared in the skim— Siegel had made sure to cut him in on the cost over-runs. So now he told Papa Louie he'd let the board know about this if there was a sitdown. Siegel was dead within 48 hours.

Lansky was incensed, he called a sitdown on Lou, who had violated his own rule that no member of the board could be hit without the board's approval.

Luciano voted with Lansky, but nobody wanted a civil war so Papa Louie was spared. He was ordered to turn over the roll to Meyer, which to save his ass he did.

And that, as they say, is what simple folks do.

If they asked me I could write a movie.

# GROWING UP
# WITH THE MOB

W hen the word filtered out that the remains of
Mr. James R. Hoffa were perhaps interred in Brother
Muscato's dump alongside the Pulaski Skyway, I gave it
the old Jersey bounce. That soil would not take a body,
I said to myself, that ground is so mean it's been reject-
ing polio for 25 years.

For two straight summers in the early 50's, I went
by it every day on the way to my ice cream route, first
in the colors of Bungalow Bar, then in the pin stripes of
Good Humor. I knew Jersey City and if I had to bury a
body there I'd pick Journal Square, where at least the
cement had some give.

Of course, with a reform administration sitting
tight in City Hall these days, even Journal Square is
out; and with hot shots running the United States
Attorney's office, how could a gangster victim rest in
peace anywhere in the Garden State?

There has been talk in recent months that things
are beginning to get back to normal in New Jersey,
after a half-dozen years of what was known by machine
politicians and Mafia bosses as "The Pogrom." Under
the leadership of United States Attorneys Fred Lacey
and Herbert Stern—now Federal judges—some 100

political figures, including mayors of Newark and Jersey City, were convicted and jailed, as well as scores of mafiosi. Suddenly nothing was as it had been; you couldn't even do business with the county leaders.

Nobody claims a return to normalcy so pervasive as to justify a top-notch burial. If, indeed, the Mob dropped Jimmy Hoffa into the dumps, it proves little more than that they were acting out of a sense of nostalgia; and if they were doing that, the Mob is not the Mob I knew as a boy.

Time was, and not so long ago at that, when it was the thing to do; it was only *proper* to bury an important personage in New Jersey. Not in the garbage heaps, never that, but in the wondrous rolling hills and lush farmlands of the Garden State.

Jersey, after all, was the sanctuary and playground of the Syndicate. We grew up understanding that, just as we learned at the breast that it was "the two parties against the people."

I never knew a kid, after kindergarten, who needed to be told that politics and crime went together. Love and marriage was a dream that became a song; the political bosses and the mob leaders were reality, and nobody thought for a second that you could have one without the other.

Nucky Johnson, the political boss of Atlantic City, hosted the country's first national crime convention on the Boardwalk in 1929. Ten years later, the Bergen County Boys welcomed onto their bosoms the top mobsters from New York, fugitives from Tom Dewey's special grand jury.

In the 1950's Johnny Kenny, the Little Guy who bossed Hudson County, had Mr. Newsboy Moriarity ensconced as the established "numbers bank" in Jersey City and environs. All of this and much more everybody knew; indeed, it was so matter of fact that if a child seemed surprised, he was marked as a hick. What still goes as sophisticated in New York came with kneepants in New Jersey.

We never talked about the Mafia, only the Syndicate. How could it be Mafia if half the mob guys we knew about were Jews and a quarter were Irish? Longy Zwillman and Doc Stacher were as big if not bigger than any gangsters in the state. Gerry Catena, who took over after Longy killed himself in his basement (*was* he a suicide?) had been Zwillman's chauffeur, and we all grew up knowing that. Harold (Kayo) Konigsberg, the erstwhile Bayonne Bomber, King of the Shylocks and executioner, was also Jewish, and it was Harold who made the last headlines about the Jersey graveyards.

In the spring of 1967, Kayo, with a 40-year stretch looking him in the eye, scared the mustaches off the people by leading F.B.I. agents to a gangland cemetery on a chicken farm near Lakewood. Lakewood! Where my grandmother and her pals used to go for the High Holidays. Where the rocking chair was the subway. Where canasta was as much action as you could expect.

The Federal agents came in with the shovels and derricks and cranes and, sure enough, they turned up two or three sacks of bones in the good earth. But no indictments, either because Konigsberg decided that he had gone about as far as he could go without turning into Abe Reles, or because his credibility was deemed less than a State Department White Paper, or because (as the cynics had it) his stuff was too hot to handle.

But it was proof enough for all of us Jersey children that what we knew with our milkshakes was good as gold. Nobody had ever come up with the remains before, but we always heard that such as Ruggiero (Richie the Boot) Biordo had a nice little incinerator right there on his estate in the Garden State.

And there were many stories about bodies being lowered in sands of our seashores. I can recall how we'd break up in grade school while singing the punch-line of *My Garden State*, which went: "I want to live and die in dear old Jersey, by the blue Atlantic shore."

In high school, the thing to do after the Junior Prom was to trip over to Ben Marden's Riviera (or by that time was it Bill Miller's Riviera?) where, along with the great Hollywood view of the Hudson, you could also see, on a cloudy night, Willie Morretti, Joe Adonis and Longy Zwillman.

That was in 1950, and shortly all of these names were household names as a result of the Kefauver hearings. Morretti, who was also known as Willie Moore, was a generous guy whom I had once had the privilege of selling haberdashery to while making after-school and Saturday Riviera money in Passaic.

He tossed me a $50 tip one afternoon to the consternation of the regular salesman, who didn't see him coming. I didn't know who he was, and when he'd come in afterwards he'd ask for "the nice Jewish kid," which drove the others crazy but ended up making me grieve when they were forced to hit him after a fine meal in Cliffside Park. It seems that Willie was as gregarious to Kefauver and Rudy Halley as to all of us and this the Mob couldn't handle. They gave him a fine funeral in Passaic.

The Mob made New Jersey its home as well as its home away from home in the mid-to-late 30's, when Tom Dewey began roughing them up in Manhattan. It was a perfect place, hard by Broadway and yet safe in the womb of the state's one-arm bandit politics, which cut neatly across party lines. They lived in mansions in Fort Lee and Cliffside Park and Englewood Cliffs. And for years they made their favorite haunt a saloon called Duke's, across the street from Palisades Amusement Park. That, plus the Riviera, made it a nice spot to live and work in.

Kefauver put a crease into the Mob's activities, but it wasn't until Lacey and Stern came along in 1969 that things got really hot. During the last few years, the Jersey Mob seemed to become a relic; like the Jersey City machine, the Newark City Hall gang, the Bergen County Boys, the Atlantic City organization, it had seemingly become an anecdote for the middle-aged.

But unlike the Rustic Cabin, the dance floor at the Meadowbrook, Duke's, the Riviera and the roller coaster at the Palisades, the Mob had not disappeared entirely. The color was gone, however, and the flush days over. And the noise we occasionally heard sounded very like a death rattle.

Jimmy Hoffa's bones may be within spitting distance of the Pulaski Skyway or a thousand miles away. What matters more is that the rumors about him were sufficient to bring back memories of the gory days in a kind of run on the collective unconscious. That, I suspect, testifies better than a room full of bugs about the way it was in dear old Jersey when corruption seemed as natural as white orchids at the Junior Prom.

# CHAMP SEGAL

□□□

Since they are not running at Saratoga nor is the heat on, why was the bar at Gallagher's bereft of heavy hitters the other night? A conundrum for sure, unless you happened to be hanging the corner of Amsterdam Av. and 76th St. at cocktail hour, which is some place to be hanging, considering that the block is dominated by the Riverside Memorial Chapel, that final Jewish solution to the ecumenical entity known as Frank E. Campbell.

Well, as it often goes in New York, the one place you don't want to be turns out to be the only place to be, and this went double at the Riverside on the night after the World Series, though even some of the smartest of the smart money set were unaware of the sad parlay going down inside the hallowed walls.

Thus, while we were on the third floor honoring the ghost of one of the grand Gallagher regulars, a man walked in and announced that Champ Segal was upstairs. "What's he doing there?" said Manny Manishor, the venerable odds-maker. "Why isn't he here paying respect to the family?" And the man said: "It wouldn't be easy, seeing as how Champ is in a similar condition to our friend lying over there in the corner."

What followed this news was a kind of Broadway shuttle, with Champ's vigil dropping downstairs and vice-versa, and everybody quite at home in both rooms, despite that our friend in the corner conducted a very different life from Mr. Harry Champ Segal.

What they had in common were the bars and race tracks of New York; otherwise, one was an eminently respectable businessman, an accusation never hurled at the Champ.

And the businessman got me to pledge, on several occasions across the years, to include him out of the papers, particularly in the unlikely event of his death. Champ loved publicity and got plenty of it, though not much lately, and no obits, which is nothing less than scandalous.

If you took only the part that could be written without that finest of adjectives, "alleged," Segal rated at least a column in *The New York Times*. Before World War I and for a couple of years after he was a bigtime boxer in all the small clubs around New York, with better than a hundred fights to his line, most of them winners.

He never won a championship, which in the way of this town explains his sobriquet, but he managed Charley Phil Rosenberg, who held the featherweight title in the 20's, plus a score of slightly lesser lights, including KO Phil Kaplan, still with us and on the spot on Champ's 78th birthday last week, which alas, had to be celebrated at the Riverside.

Add to all this his bloodline—his older brother Sam invented the jimmyproof Segal Lock—and you've got the makings of a Page One sendoff. Which, come to think of it, Champ would have had, if he stuck with the family business dynasty.

But what kind of person would squander his life on corporate affairs, when out there for the pickings were such giants as Arnold Rothstein, Bugsy Siegel, Owney Madden, Frank Costello, Lepke Buchalter, Niggy Rutkin, Longy Zwillman, Doc Stacher, Lucky Luciano, Meyer Lansky, and name your Hall of Fame?

Obviously, the Segal Lock Company was no contest, and with minor exceptions at the end of his glorious career at the bar sinister, neither were the forces of law and order. When we consider that the Champ's rap sheet dates to 1917, and includes arrests for murder, mutiny on the high seas (yes indeed), shylocking, bookmaking, and contempt of court—for all of which he did maybe a year in *durance vile*—it's apparent that we are talking about a presence who is right now negotiating his way to heaven, where, after all there are no wiretap transcripts.

His biggest trouble was in 1939, when a Los Angeles grand jury indicted him for aiding and abetting the murder of Harry (Big Greenie) Greenberg. His codefendants in that one were Lepke, Bugsy Siegel, and Frankie Carbo. The story with it was that Big Greenie had been making noises about turning state's evidence on Lepke, then in hiding from the DA's Murder, Inc. investigation.

Greenie was spotted in Hollywood, where Bugsy Siegel held sway and where Champ ran a fashionable barber shop that perhaps handled some wagers in the bargain. So the contract went to the Bug, who gave the gun to Carbo who took out Greenberg, allegedly. And allegedly, Champ was the wheelman, meaning the guy who drove one of the torpedoes to the airport.

Of course, nothing ever happened, unless you count the electrocution of Lepke five years later on different and surely less substantial grounds.

But nothing happened to Champ, who if he ran to the form I knew, wasn't so much as fazed. Indeed, the only time I ever saw him upset was when Frank Costello gave him up, and he wasn't upset with Costello, he was upset with me.

In the spring of 1970, Segal was arrested on charges of running a million-dollar wire room out of his apartment. The fingerman was none other than the great Frank C., who was now accusing him of booking his action.

I ran into Champ that night and said, "Well, it's very nice that your old pal turns out to be an informer." Champ answered, "Don't give me that stuff. Frank wouldn't do that to me, never. Frank's class, don't give me he's a rat bastard, I'll belt you."

I showed him the headline: "Costello Blows The Whistle On His Bookie." Lies, said the Champ, and walked away. But it was true, and after that I didn't see too much of Segal, though he somehow avoided the slammer once again, no thanks to Frank C.

The last time I talked to him, he was doing a "Ping-Pong" bit—small and light—at Rikers Island, owing to a contempt conviction arising out of an alleged loan-shark thing. It was a couple of years ago, and I was trying some criminal cases and so had a client living at Rikers. The client called me from jail, wondering when I was going to spring him, and surprised me by putting Champ on the phone.

"Listen," Champ said in a whisper, "don't get this bum bail 'til I get out, Y'hear?"

Why?

"He's a terrific cook, he makes the best guinea food I ever tasted, and I tasted plenty. If he goes I'm back to slop, so don't make no fancy moves, leave him be, he's okay. It's only a couple of weeks, so just do me this one. Make it a favor, I'll make it up to you."

Champ got out first, anyhow, and last week he got away, and now who's going to make it up to me?

# ISRAEL SCHAWARZBERG

As it has each year since that morning in 1970 when the bells rang on him, there will appear tomorrow on the death page of *The New York Times*, the following:

ISRAEL SCHAWARZBERG, REMEMBRANCE AND RESPECT FROM FRIENDS AND ENEMIES.

Tomorrow night—in honor or in spite, in sorrow or in joy—remnants of the old Jewish Mob will raise the tea glasses to Schawarzberg at such diverse cusineries as Shmulky Bernstein's, Ratner's, and Lou G. Siegel's.

"Well of course and why not?" said Alias Joey Kleinshiker, the once, present, and future right arm of Israel Schawarzberg. "He is loved and hated in equal proportion by friends and enemies alike, so why shouldn't they toast him on the anniversary of his alleged death?"

Joey Kleinshiker, who in English translation is Little Joey, does not accept the coroner's verdict on his leader, despite that he picked his coffin and is responsible for the annual memorial announcements in the paper.

"Israel is too big for life, and is in such a hurry to live it that one day his body runs out on him," Joey said. "What has that got to do with death? I don't make a move without consulting with him. Why, do you?"

Well of course not. Who could know Izzy Schawarzberg and still believe that death is a silencer?

He ran against the law for more than 40 of his 56 years on earth, with as many lives as he had aliases. On police blotters from the precinct house to Interpol he was a/k/a Mizo, Irving Ace, Irving Ticket, Fat Tiger and Mr. Israel.

He would never qualify for the Mount Rushmore of crime, but he was the last great single-o act in the American underworld, an entrepreneur in a game gone soft with corporate-style bureaucracy.

He pioneered the college basketball fix, and in his spare time he fixed horses, cops and witnesses. He swindled banks and shylocks and mafiosi. He made book and took off bookmakers.

In his various stints behind bars he developed into the most famous jailhouse lawyer of his time, boasting a record of 29 wins for 32 writs brought on behalf of fellow prisoners.

On the outside he invoked an ancient statute to become certified—despite his prison record—as a law clerk by the New York Court of Appeals, and he used his mob connections to build up a flourishing practice that became the bane of Federal and state prosecutors.

This career lasted seven raucous years, ending only when the Feds pinned a rap on him and the lady lawyer he worked for, convicting them of trying to suborn a witness in a narcotics trial. He represented himself and succeeded in gaining acquittal on all but one charge of conspiracy.

His speech at sentencing was by common consent of the organized bar the greatest in the history of jurisprudence. Alluding to his codefendant, the lawyer who had just received two years, he said: "Your honor, I'm shocked beyond recall that you could give this poor woman a deuce. After all, your honor, I'm innocent. But she's *really* innocent."

I met him 15 years ago, in my incarnation as a *New York Post* reporter, and covered him until his alleged end. He was easily the best copy in the city, and never better than on the day a bomb turned up under his car, parked peacefully in the Bronx.

The bomb was a crude affair spotted by a neighbor who notified the cops, who in turn told Schawarzberg. It made the network news, and that night he drove down to his birthplace on the Lower East Side to prove to his pals he was "standing pat." It was necessary for him to show no fear, but he wasn't about to start the car. He called the Automobile Assn. claiming he couldn't get it going.

"The AAA guy naturally turned it right over," he said. It's a good thing he didn't see me holding my ears across the street. After that, I called them every day, why should I take chances? But after a week they wouldn't come anymore, they figured I was crazy."

So he tapped alias Joey Kleinshiker, who owed him for having been sprung out of Dannemora on a Schawarzberg writ years before.

"After three weeks, I couldn't take it," Joey told

me. "Each morning I'd turn over the motor, but nothing ever happened."

Not much happened to Izzy after his celebrated arrest, in 1951, for fixing the Manhattan College basketball team. It was the first break in the long-rumored college hoop scandal, but somehow Schawarzberg drew only a year on a misdemeanor plea.

"I let them know I'd blow the whistle on other Catholic schools," he said. "Does Cardinal Spellman have clout in this town, are you kidding?"

# WHO'S CRAZY NOW?

Dutch Schultz and David Berkowitz wouldn't connect in the average name-association game, though they had certain surface attributes in common.

Each in his time was Public Enemy Number One and each in his way was considered screwy by contemporaries. Schultz was known as the Crazy Dutchman, and, of course, the alleged "Son of Sam" is thought to be off the wall by everyone except the courts.

Schultz was born Arthur Flegenheimer, the son of German-Jewish immigrants. Berkowitz was born Richard David Falco, an illegitimate child adopted in infancy by the Berkowitzes, who raised him.

Flegenheimer converted to Catholicism on his death-bed. Berkowitz found Jesus in his middle 20's.

Coincidence to be sure, and hardly worthy of mention if not for the motion last week by Son of Sam's lawyers to move his murder trial upstate.

It's hard to imagine what difference it could make in the life of David Berkowitz whether he is tried in Brooklyn or the Borscht Belt — or if he's tried at all — but the change of venue effort serves to remind us of Dutch Schultz, who 43 years ago this week changed his own venue by giving himself up in Syracuse.

He was the most wanted man in the country in 1934.

During Prohibition, he had been the great Beer Baron and, in the early 30's, he organized the Harlem numbers racket, plus a fierce restaurant and taxicab hustle.

Nobody knows how many people he killed and ordered blown away during his halcyon days. Thanks to sweet connections with Tammany Hall, the Dutchman was never indicted for any such pecadillos.

In January 1933, however, the Feds charged him with tax evasion. Schultz did not show up for the arraignment, on the apparently sound grounds that the advent of Franklin Roosevelt would put Tammany back in the saddle and save him the annoyance of a trial.

For nearly a year, Schultz went on running his rackets and running all around town as if nothing had happened. But in November '34, a triple-play combination—made up of J. Edgar Hoover, Mayor Fiorello LaGuardia and Treasury Secretary Henry Morgenthau—turned him into the hottest ticket in the country.

The Dutchman ordered his lawyers to find a place he could be tried outside Manhattan, where the publicity would surely cook him. They turned up Syracuse, which was within the Albany district, where Schultz—a Bronx resident—was supposed to have paid his taxes.

The Dutchman held wondrous press conferences there and managed to get a hung jury, despite an airtight Government case. But the Feds weren't through with him; they scheduled another trial in Malone, near the Canadian border.

The Dutchman arrived in Malone a week before the trial like a presidential candidate come to Convention City. He threw a party at the dance hall and invited the whole town, and nearly everybody came.

"We find the defendant not guilty," said the foreman and the crowded courtroom cheered.

It won't happen to David Berkowitz.

A year later, the Crazy Dutchman was cut down by Syndicate guns in Newark and that won't happen to Berkowitz either.

# II

SALOON SONGS

# SINGALONG SAM

I was 17 when I stepped up to the door at Sardi's for the first time, and guess who was stepping out? Only Noel Coward in black tie, with Marlene Dietrich on his arm. I knew then and there that when I grew up I'd never stray far from Sardi's bar, where obviously they didn't break the promise to the hope.

In my early 30's, fortune and circumstance landed me practically on the corner bar stool. I fast discovered that the one thing you were not going to do at Sardi's was grow up, and if you knew how to do it you didn't need to grow old, either. We used to say, those pictures on the walls don't get any older, why should we?

What put me on the premises was a job I got reporting for *The New York Times*, right next door. That trip began in 1965, and for the five merry years that followed, I logged about as much time in Sardi's as at the paper.

What brings this to the fore suddenly is a brand new coffee table picture book featuring the famous caricatures that adorn the place, appropriately titled *Off The Wall at Sardi's*, put together lovingly by Vincent Sardi Jr. and Thomas Edward West, with an accompanying memoir by the boss.

I told Vincent I'd review it, but why tell *his* Sardi's stories when I can tell mine? You can buy his, and you should: It's a cameo history of the Broadway theater, the pictures are wonderful, it's a perfect holiday gift, it's published by Applause and it's yours for $39.95. That's the plug, and I mean it. And now sit back and listen to *my* Sardi's stories, which if Vincent knew he would never tell, and how would he know as he did not do too much hanging around the bar with us flies.

A tale of Two Christmases, first.

It was a blistery night out there, 20-odd years ago, and so naturally we were huddled up around Johnnie Walker at the Little Bar, which fronted Sardi's in those days. The Little Bar looked right out on 44th Street. A couple of actors were there—Robert Preston, Roland Winters—and a host of regulars, including the Brothers Repp and the Brothers Karp, and of course the ubiquitous Tony August, known only as Tony A.

It was not a night unlike all the others, except that a guy was buying drinks for the bar in honor of his wife's birthday, only his wife was home cooking, nor was his mistress around. Well, nobody asks any questions when a man is buying and indeed everybody toasted the missing wife with great sincerity, and only one citizen mentioned the mistress.

Tony A., formerly of the defunct *Daily Mirror*, directed my attention to the window, where behold there was a nose pressing up against, and behind the nose a lean face that resembled Robert Q. Lewis, though it was hardly likely that Robert Q. Lewis, the TV limelight, would be pressing his nose against the window of Sardi's Little Bar, or maybe any other window for that matter.

Anyway, Tony A. waves to the nose as if to say, "Come right in," and the next thing we know here is the Robert Q. Lewis guy in the bar, smiling and thanking us all with a singsong style. "Thank you all of you here thank you very very much it is such a pleasure to see such a nice crowd on so freezing a night thank you so much." Like he was singing "The Old Mill Stream"—that was the delivery.

George Repp, who looked like George Brent, and who had done a few bit parts in Hollywood in his heyday, made room for this guy immediately and I saw the gleam in his eye, he had a real one, it said. Nobody could spot a sucker like George Repp, who after all didn't have the wherewithal to live the life he deserved, so he did the best he could, which was very good at that.

Another hour went by and then another and soon it was closing time and this guy, whom we eventually called Singalong Sam, grabbed the check, right out of the hands of the man whose wife we were toasting. This check was $149.80, I remember it well, and today it would mean a grand. George Repp's eyes shined.

Twice a week, Singalong Sam would show up and soon he was taking George Repp to the tables for dinner. George hadn't eaten at Sardi's for 30 years, but now he was the host. He'd invite half the bar, and Singalong Sam was only too happy to pay, always in cash. One night I got into the act, and when I ordered chicken salad, George glowered at me. "Take the prime beef," he said. "It's delicious. And order soup!"

The year went by pleasantly in this manner and then, on another cold night near yuletide, a woman in a hooded coat walked into the Little Bar. Singalong Sam was happily buying us nightcaps. She approached him, she grabbed him by the throat, she said: "You bastard! So this is where you're spending all our money!"

"Meet my wife," he said, to the tune of "Make Believe."

Her answer was to drag him by the throat.

But he held on. He said, "Wait my dear, wait a minute. I have unfinished business. The check! Ray, please, my check!"

He paid it, too, and I don't want to know what he paid when she got him home. We never saw him again.

Tony A. said: "God brought him to us on Christmas and God took him from us on Christmas."

Tony A. used the bar for an office after the *Mirror* went under. He got all his calls there, and once Vincent Sardi picked up the phone and said, "Hello, Tony August's residence."

I did as Tony A. did near the end of my days at *The Times.* I decided to start a new magazine, *Scanlan's Monthly*, with Warren Hinckle, the founder of *Ramparts.* I couldn't use *The Times* to raise the money and we didn't have the money to open an office. So we used Sardi's bar.

But one day the phones went kerflooey there and stayed kerflooey the next night. We ran an ad, one of those small print jobs, on the front page of *The Times*: "Telephone Company! Please fix the phones at Sardi's Bar. Signed, *Scanlan's Monthly.*"

The following morning at 8, a half-dozen repairmen were in the joint—they woke Vincent Sardi for this—and we were back in business. When Leonard Lyons showed up on his regular rounds during lunch that day, I told him the story and he used it as the lead item in his *New York Post* column, you could look it up.

Oh, there are going to be people mad at me for all the stories I am leaving out, but I think as many will be relieved, because I could stir up a lot of trouble here if I had the space, even if I stick with my days on *The Times*.

But it is Christmas and I would not use them anyhow. I will tell only one story that happened after I left the Gray Lady.

Mickey Cohen was in town to hustle his autobiography, it was 1975, and I arranged to meet the Wild Jew Boy at Sardi's for lunch.

He was a has-been, of course, and had been for years, since Bobby Kennedy sent him to Alcatraz on a tax rap, where a crazed inmate took a lead pipe to his head, leaving him a cripple.

But he pulled up to Sardi's in a limo, he managed to walk with a cane, and the great Jimmy, the maitre d', treated him as if he was still Mickey Cohen of Sunset Strip.

People by the gross stopped by during lunch, everybody wanted to shake the hand of the hand that whacked out who knew who and who cared how many. Among them was a *Times* editor.

"That sonofabitch!" I said.

"Why?" asked Mickey Cohen.

"He's cut me dead for years and suddenly he's all honey."

"What's he do?"

"He's an editor."

Mickey Cohen smiled benevolently.

"Never call a man a sonofabitch who's in a walk of life that calls for him to be a sonofabitch."

# NOONDAY SUN? ONLY FOR MAD DOGS AND JOGGERS

In the little cabaret atop the Russian Tea Room, on Noël Coward's birthday, a young lady gazed at the packed house, shook her head in awe, and said to her boyfriend: "Isn't it amazing the way people go out late in New York?"

This was a couple of Sundays ago, a few ticks before 11, with everybody sipping drinks while waiting for Steve Ross to light up the old beauties in the Coward canon.

My wife winked at me, hearing this kid go on about what night people we New Yorkers were. A half-hour earlier, a neighbor had looked at *us* in awe, all dressed up to go dancing and here it is 10:30. "What a great thing, to go out at this hour," the neighbor said, as she ran off to catch the video store before it closed.

It turned out that the girl in the cabaret was from Washington, D.C., which of course goes a long way toward explaining *her* awe factor.

"If it's 11 o'clock in New York, what time is it in Washington?" I couldn't resist asking.

She laughed. "Once the sun goes down, it's always 4 o'clock in the morning in Washington," she said.

This *mot* lit up my soul, even before Steve Ross could swing into "Mad Dogs and Englishmen." I am, you see, ever on the hunt for signs that wit and joy live in the young. After all, if Shirley MacLaine is right, if we are doomed to return to this blood-soaked world, one would like to believe that there will be someone around to have fun with.

Unfortunately, in my cockeyed optimism, I made the mistake of casing the room for others like this twentysomething lass and her lad; alas, nobody there remotely under 40, and now all I could do was to smile wanly as Mr. Ross gave us "Someday I'll Find You."

But in the morning, no. In the morning, I was determined to spend the rest of the holiday season dodging the sun in an effort to recall the legendary New York night life of my wasted youth, so that I could bring some taste of it to my loyal following out there, all of whom (in my mind's eye) desperately hunger for tales of the way it was before the Fitness Fascists, the Smoke Fascists and the Booze Fascists broke all those lights along the Great White Way.

To give you a quick idea, the only surprise anybody would have registered upon seeing me leaving my apartment at 10:30 was that I was still home at that hour. In the early 60's, when I first lived in Manhattan, 11 o'clock wasn't even the shank of the night. Hey, there was the 2 o'clock show at Basin Street East, the Duke's in town, and to Clarke's, and if we were still movable, the Brasserie.

Once you start thinking about those days, something good always happens. On the morning after Coward's birthday bash, Jack Whitaker phoned to in-

vite me to lunch "with a few good guys" at the Grand
Hyatt. This is hardly the usual venue for the Silver Fox,
the king of the sportscasters, who when in town is
likely to be sighted at "21" or Neary's or Gallagher's or
Clarke's.

But I ask no questions when Jack Whitaker calls,
for I know that there is guaranteed to be good stories,
good liquor and sundown before the camaraderie calls
it a day. No wine spritzers before lunch, we're talking
Beefeater and Johnnie Black and Absolut, are you kidding? I mean, how you going to get the shoulders
down, how you going to get the conversation flowing,
c'mon, white wine never did that for nobody nohow.

Mr. Whitaker is holding court at the bar when I
arrive, 20 minutes late and a shooter behind. And the
court is composed of some of the best talkers of the
second half of the 20th century.

Here's Jim Lowe, formerly Mr. Broadway of
WNEW and perhaps the future Mr. Broadway of
WQEW, once the folks who run the new Sinatra-Ella
station get their feet on the ground and notice that
what they need to keep the music going is alive and
well and living in East Hampton.

And we have Irwin Hasen, creator of *Dondi*, and
Johnny Angel, creator of Johnny Angel, and Neary of
Neary's Pub, and Tony Rolfe of Sulzberger-Rolfe, your
eternal landlord, and the eternal of the eternals, Danny
Lavezzo, Grand Boniface of P.J. Clarke's and therefore
of what is left of the saloon world that was once New
York, New York.

"You remember Ed Wilcox?" Danny Lavezzo says.

Ed Wilcox, with Liz Smith, practically wrote the

Cholly Knickerbocker column, bylined Igor Cassini, in the old *Journal-American*.

One night at Clarke's (Mr. Lavezzo recalls), Frank Gifford and Kyle Rote got the call to nature at the same time. While they were in the johnnie, the waiter came for drink orders. Wilcox said, "See what the backs in the boy's room will have."

"I walked into my joint late one night after a dinner party in black tie," Danny Lavezzo said. "And Wilcox took one look at me and asked, 'What happened, did Kelso die?'"

Frankie Ribando, recovering from a stroke now, controlled the invisible rope to the back room at Clarke's like a regular Ayatollah, for decades. Wilcox said that Frankie looked like "the conductor on the Lionel train."

Tony Rolfe said that he now had in his possession the seating list for the last dinner, June 23, 1959, at Toots Shor's original joint, 51 West 51st Street. I was there only once, but I remember it as a warm place, quite different from the helicopter port Tootsie opened a couple of years later around the block.

"One night at the old Tootsie's," Danny Lavezzo said, "the lights flickered over the bar. And Bob Considine, without missing a sip, said: 'They just electrocuted the chef.'"

I was intrigued with that seating list, and the next day Tony Rolfe faxed it to me. Here's a partial dais: Jackie Gleason, Eddie Arcaro, John Wayne, Leo Durocher, Jack Dempsey, Don Ameche and Jack E. Leonard. Space forbids me to list the guys who didn't make the cut for the dais. But try Jim Farley, Walter Cronkite and Wellington Mara.

Not to be denied, I told my Sinatra-Tootsie story. One night in the 40's, Toots demanded that Frank show early for dinner. Waiting at the bar for him were Bing Crosby, Jack Dempsey and Babe Ruth. "What's this, a frame-up?" Frank Sinatra asked Tootsie. "Bet your ass," said Shor. He walked the four of them through the room to the rear table, and the room stood up and applauded.

This doesn't happen on white wine, baby.

Nor will it produce this one, which I picked up late that same night at Elaine's, the soul survivor of the great nightspots. A Larry Hart lyric to "Bewitched," that never made it to the *Pal Joey* score:

"When your dreamboat is leaking/and your pal ain't your pal

Geometrically speaking/just keep him verti-cal."

Noël Coward died too soon. Only mad dogs and joggers go out in the noonday sun.

# Sobriety: a Dangerous Thing?

*"June, July, August—there goes the summer!"*
— Mrs. Louis B. Mayer

One of New York's finest saloon raconteurs was finally prevailed upon by his better half, and so spent most of the summer at the Hazelden Foundation in Center City, Minn., the Parris Island of detox. He was sorely missed by the thin corps of sun-dodgers manning the Broadway bistro barricades, and early returns from the home front indicate that he may be missed for a long time and maybe forever—alas, not only by his old drinking pals.

The minute the guy got back from Hazelden, he told his wife as follows: "I am leaving you, honey."

Perhaps because he added the endearment, she kept right on hugging him, saying how clear his eyes were and how wonderful he looked.

"I'll pack my bags now. I should be out of here in an hour."

"What?" she said. "Are you serious?"

"Absolutely."

"Why?"

"Look," he said, patiently. "I didn't like you too much when I was drunk. Now that I'm sober, I hate you."

Like love, Johnnie Walker has his reason, which reason knows not why. When spouses and other well-wishers forget this truth, they are likely to end up singing Cousin Joe's blues: "You got what you wanted, but you lost what you had."

Maybe the Surgeon General should put a warning sign on every bar and every bottle: "Sobriety may be dangerous to what got you this far."

In our Lion's Head days in the Village 20 years ago, Doug Ireland spotted me drinking seltzer three nights hand-running. A doctor had lied to me about my lipid count, thinking it could only do me good to live without; what did I need booze for?

"Are you O.K.?" Douglas said.

"I'm on the wagon."

"The wagon? How do you get your shoulders down?"

I ordered a double Gibson and I've been keeping them down ever since.

Naturally, if you can't drink, you can't drink. I'm not knocking Hazelden or Alcoholics Anonymous or any of these other joints. But if you like it and if the liver says go, don't let the docs or the civilian health fascists scare you into becoming a white wine, dinner-at-7 bore. Join us sun-dodgers, in all seasons! I was practically a beach bum as a kid, but once they air-conditioned the bars . . .

# DON'T BLAME
# JOHNNIE WALKER

ם ם ם

**M**itchell Parish called me to have a couple of drinks the other night. This to me was stardust, which Mitchell Parish wrote, and just in time, which he didn't write. The thing was, I was having the blues when Mitchell Parish called, and right away I knew I wasn't going to have the blues no more.

Of course I'm going to explain this, are you kidding?

When Mitchell Parish rang me up I was down in the depths with Anna Quindlen. I have always considered Anna Quindlen a good writer and a right broad, but here was Anna Quindlen in *The New York Times* newspaper beating hell out of Johnnie Walker and, while she was at it, out of Philip Morris.

It is Anna Quindlen's opinion that what this country needs is for everybody to turn drinkers into pariahs the way we have done to smokers.

And here was Mitchell Parish, at 91, asking me for drinks at Neary's pub on 57th and First. "Make it 7:30," he said, and we'll "throw down a few shooters."

Mitchell Parish, who wrote "Sophisticated Lady" with Duke Ellington and that great theme line: "Smoking, drinking, never thinking of tomorrow."

My daddy taught me never to argue with a person who makes 90, and my Uncle Hen taught me never to blame Johnnie Walker. My father never drank much but smoked 15 cigars a day and died of something else at 81. My Uncle Hen smoked 60 Luckies a day and drank a quart of Johnnie Black and only lived to be 76. His brothers never drank or smoked—and never made it to 60.

"When I go, do me a favor," my Uncle Hen said to me the year before he passed. "Put the Johnnie label on my stone and write under it, 'If it wasn't for him, I'd have been here a whole lot earlier.'"

The Surgeon General will of course insist that these people are "anecdotal," but I'll lay plenty of 50–1 that no Surgeon General will live as long or as good as Manny Manishor, who is still with us at 93. We threw Manny a 90th birthday party at Gallagher's bar, and he made us all stand for three hours while he smoked Pall Mall regulars and drank Red Label with one peg of ice.

Manny Manishor was then the reigning odds-maker on Broadway, and would likely still be, had not one of his family decided that he was spending too much money on booze and women and so sent him to a nursing home. On that glorious night of his 90th, however, he was approached by a young guy of, say, 60 from Cleveland who stood on the outskirts of the crowd of regulars and finally said he couldn't take it anymore.

"Sir," he said, "what is the secret?"

Manny tapped his glass, which said buy me first, kid, and when the guy did it right, Manny lit up a fresh cig, blew it at the guy's face and said: "It's easy, pal. Abuse yourself in every way. But never eat fried."

The Health Fascists, like the Surgeon General, will have nothing of this, I don't have to tell you. They are feeling the wind at their backs and are hellbent, or is it heaven-bent? They will not be satisfied until the world is smoke-free and booze-free. If that means fun-free, so what? So let me be form-free for a moment.

Joe Frisco, the late stuttering comic, was walking down Fifth Avenue one day when he saw Raymond Massey on the other side of the street. Mr. Massey had played Abe Lincoln for so long that he practically looked like him, and he was strutting as if he had the pipe hat on.

Joe Frisco took one look and said, "He woo-oo-oon't be sa-a-a-atis-fied until he's assa-a-a-ssinated."

Well, we have to fight back.

And bus stops. The other morning, while going for my bagel—are bagels still O.K.?—I heard a woman tell a guy to kill his cig on the corner of 90th and Broadway. Now here were trucks and buses running by exuding fumes right in that lady führer's face. But this lousy little Marlboro Light was going to send her to an early grave.

Of course, what gave the Smoke Fascists the "right" to drive us crazy and off the streets and even out of the bars was the "secondary smoke" business. This stuff was set up by a bunch of academic doctors who played with numbers to put across an ideological position. And we have the equivalent of civil war, thereby. Listen, now. At worst, 25 percent of three-pack-a-day smokers die of lung cancer. So how can they prove a thing about secondary smoke?

The next thing we know, they'll have No Smoking signs on the panhandlers' cups.

But Anna Quindlen started with the demon rum, so let's have another drink.

What actuated Ms. Quindlen's column was an incident in East Aurora, N.Y. In that upstate town, a high school quarterback was caught drinking a beer at a picnic by (of all people) an assistant coach, who deemed it his obligation to turn the kid in to the principal. The boy was suspended from the team, whereupon his father turned in seven other players similarly guzzling the Budweiser. The school gave its version of equal protection: Everybody got kicked off the team. And now the father of the quarterback has sued the school board for denying his kid and the others of their careers, which is to say college scholarships.

Ms. Quindlen is shocked at this lawsuit. And I thought she'd be shocked at the crazy school board, but what do I know. As I said, I always thought she was a right broad, for which language I am sure to suffer, even as I'm sure Ms. Quindlen knows I mean the very best and certainly no ill.

What comes out of all this is that Prohibition, which Ring Lardner said was "better than no booze at all," would be back again if it hadn't already been tried. And in a real way is coming back through the side door of driving and athletics.

The cops sit outside saloons and grab people practically before they start their cars. The kids are the primary targets and, don't get me wrong, I'm not for drunken driving.

But going after the young people, making them a class that can't be trusted, will only make them trust us less. It is altogether outrageous to tell them that they are old enough to fight for their country but not mature enough to down a beer.

In New York City, very few kids have cars or even driving licenses. Yet they can't drink until they are 21. If we are not just punishing them for being young, why not let them choose between a license and a drink? If they don't drive, let them do what the hell they want, don't forbid them booze.

But what we have here is old-fashioned moralism dressed up in the usual we're-doing-this-for-you-honey clothing. It's bound to turn them against us and bound to fail for, like all prohibition, it will not work and will only encourage more drinking and more smoking.

And now the sports pages are filled with columns that sound like Billy Sunday with a new twist. Why should we allow ballplayers to drink if they can't use crack?

All I can say is, I miss the Great Bambino more than ever. He trained on Johnnie Walker like my Uncle Hen, and sometimes there's no other way to get your shoulders down.

# THE CIGAR CRISIS

ooo

W e are the true American pariahs, we 400,000 aficionados of fine cigars. They run us out of restaurants, harangue us on the streets and often drive us out of our own living rooms. It has become so noxious, or at least so obvious, that even *Newsweek*, that paragon of the mainstream, has declared that we are "ripe for rebellion."

To which I say: Yes, but.

Yes, our frustration level is at fail safe from the relentless battering ram of the smoke fascists. Yes, our anger rises with every raid on our wallets by politicians so shameless as to subject us to "sin" taxes. Yes, we are made to suffer the unspeakable insult of being barred from places where cigarettes are welcome. And yes, the outrage supreme: Cigarette junkies ordering us to kill the Davidoff!

But.

Unless we have the will to fight, the problems of 400,000 cigar lovers won't amount to a hill of beans in this New World Order.

If we are content with grousing among ourselves, comparing horror stories at fancy smokers, playing Jiggs to Maggie at home and Casper Milquetoast in restaurants, we will go the way of the Armenians to the Turks, without even a Saroyan to document our days of pleasure.

But if we can harness our heat and turn it into a plan of battle, we will not only stand off the fascists, we stand a real chance of winning the war. Because we are right.

Of course, the first thing is to believe we are right.

Sadly, too many of us have lost that belief. We think that the fascists are fanatics, but on the other hand maybe they have a point. Cigar people never put it that way—I know guys who would invite me outside for suggesting it—but you don't have to be Dr. Freud to figure out that there's more to this prevailing passivity than the party line that we are, after all, gentlemen, and gentlemen abhor scenes.

Here are selected scenes from my many years in the trenches.

A wealthy publisher invites me to dinner at his penthouse. From past experience, I know not to take my poor little $3 panatelas. This man was getting Cohibas delivered to his door during the Bay of Pigs, and they are delivered now, along with the Monte Cristo's. An evening with this aficionado is like a night with Cole Porter during the reign of the Rolling Stones.

But at cocktails, no cigar. On the second martini, I get up my nerve. "Have you stopped smoking?" I say.

"My daughter-in-law," he says. "She'll leave if we light up. Please, don't say anything. After dinner, we'll go to the study, just you and me."

At Le Club, I offer a Bolivar Royal Corona to a leader of industry. He slips it into his black tie. "Wonderful," he says. "I'll smoke it at home tonight." Well let's do it now, I say. "No, no, they'll be trouble." This is a private party and he is afraid to light up in front of people who would give three fingers to have his business.

I am at the bar in a fancy French restaurant in Manhattan. I pull out a Punch Rothschild. The man next to me, a major figure in the newspaper world, says: "Are you going to smoke it here?" You bet, says I. He is incredulous. "I was walking in Central Park the other day," he says, "and a woman jumped at me. 'Put that stink-bomb out,' she said. It's a real reign of terror," he said. I asked him what he did about it. "Well, uh, well I, uh, well what could I do?"

Most people hate cigar smokers without reason. I love them without reason. So I didn't say what I should have said: "You can act like a man! You don't have to wimp off, like you're committing a crime."

When did the robbery take place? When did we, the once-proud legatees of Winston Churchill, Groucho Marx, John F. Kennedy, W.C. Fields, George Gershwin, George Burns, Mark Twain—when did we turn into closet smokers?

I think that we have been mesmerized, against our finest instincts, by the unrelenting assault of the Health Brigade, those neo-Prohibitionists who will not rest until all civilized pleasure is removed from the world.

It is time to fight back, time to ring out in thunder that we are right and they are wrong.

The Surgeon General, against all the winds that blow, has never proclaimed that cigar smoking is dangerous to health. But how many people know this? Even cigar aficionados are surprised to hear it, I find.

And I find that it is one of our greatest weapons against the fascists.

Depending on my mood, I say a lot of different things when someone asks me to "put that thing out." On the beach in Fire Island last summer, a guy ordered it — they never ask, as you know — and I noted that here we were on the sea and how could he? "My wife," he said. "It bothers my wife." They always put it on the little woman.

"Well let her ask me," I said.

She was more diffident. "Would you please put it out?" she said.

"I will," I said.

They smiled and walked away.

"Wait!"

"Yes?"

"You have a choice."

"What do you mean?" said the hubbie.

"I'll put it out in your eye or hers."

They took off like wide receivers on the Miami Dolphins.

At Sardi's upstairs bar the other day, I found myself two bodies away from perfume that you could smell in Hoboken. I was about to run downstairs when the guy accompanying this sweet-smelling lady told me to put out the cigar.

"We're at a bar, pal," I said.

"It bothers her," he said.

"O.K.," I said. "I'll make a deal with you."

"What deal?"

"You give her a bath and I'll put out the cigar."

He leaned at me for a second, trying to look bad. And then he took the lady by the arm and said, "C'mon honey, let's go to a place where there are *gentlemen*."

Gentlemen prefer cigars, we all know that. But I think we also know that most gentlemen would have put out the cigar. That's why the gentleman is a dope.

We will never get it right until we go back to first principles and understand that *they* are the vulgarians, they violate propriety, they are the shameless who insist that everyone bow to their command.

They are also the bullies in the schoolyard, and like all bullies they back down when they see the face of courage.

The same will go for the restaurateurs, if we use our power. Cigar people are the biggest spenders in the world, and when we are on the town, we're the prime customers of the best restaurants. And they have the gall to tell us that we can't smoke here. "I'm sorry, sir, cigar smoking is not permitted."

Walk out when they do that. Just walk out with your party, and see what happens. I lay 12–7 that they call you back on the spot. And 20–1 that they change their policy the next day.

I tried the following one night and it worked in a hurry.

A friend was setting up a party at a Village club. I said, "Find out if they allow cigars." He called back. "They say no."

I called the joint and ordered a table for twelve. The captain was delighted, eager to please my every whim for what table and what time. Then I said, "By the way, are cigars permitted?" Uh, no sir. "Cancel it," I said.

The next few days I had my friends call the place, women and men, ordering tables from four to fourteen. And then asking about cigars. And cancelling. They immediately opened the bar to us, and today the world.

But I refuse to leave you thinking that I am promoting a defensive war only. Let me take you to the Hunt Room at '21', a half a humidor ago.

It's a wedding party, thirtysomething. Nobody is smoking, not a Marlboro Lite in sight. I light up a Macanudo Hyde Park Cafe.

A lanky brunette approaches.

"I want you," she says.

"Say what?"

"You're the only man here."

"Why?"

"You have the gorgeous nerve to smoke a cigar."

\* \* \*

This piece was written to order for *Cigar Aficionado*. The new magazine threw a black-tie launch party in September 1992 on the St. Regis roof. I gave an impromptu talk that was nothing less than a call to arms. It brought the crowd to its feet. The publisher, Marvin Shanken, hugged me and asked if I could write it up for his next issue, deadline one week. I delivered on time—hell I could have written it that night—but straightaway trouble began.

Gordon Mott, the editor, gave me one of those *phumphes* that 30 years in the pits against these types made me jot death on my notepad as he explained that Mr. Shanken would of course have to read it, and Mr. Shanken was traveling, of course, and of course we therefore have to miss this particular edition which anyway was full up, ahem, and of course it would not matter as of course with perhaps a slight bit of softening the piece would appear in the next number, which of course was in March for of course we are publishing a quarterly of course and of course not to worry.

A couple of months went by before Mr. Mott announced that Mr. Shanken considered the piece "too tough for our readers." I pointed out that I had written exactly what I promised and what Mr. Shanken wanted, and furthermore that he, Mr. Mott, had told me to be as "tough" as my speech. Of course, this went nowhere, whereupon I demanded money whereupon he said, "You did this on spec." Whereupon I said a few things I would prefer my mother not read here, and repeated same to Mr. Shanken, who said he would think it over. There would have to be changes, but maybe the piece could run.

A month or so later, he killed it outright on the grounds that it was too "militaristic." I had to threaten him with a law suit to get a lousy kill fee out of it all, and the next time I do a piece on cheapskates, Marvin Shanken goes in the lead.

Anyway, I mentioned this situation to Peter Bloch, the editor of Penthouse, and Peter said, "Fax it to me." Five minutes later he bought the piece. Put that in your cigar, Marvie boy.

□□□

# REACHING FROM A CHECK

□□□

In the pantheon of the parsimonious rich, few stood taller than Fred MacMurray, who got away the other day in Hollywood with the moths still working on his 1935 unzipped Hickok wallet. Way down there in his long obit, *The New York Times* allowed as how he was "frugal," which is like calling David Duke a moderate.

Joe E. Lewis, the great saloon comic, used to say of such guys, "He's got a impediment in his reach." The world is full of them, the penurious people, and they don't have to be very rich to qualify, just comfortable. There's one in every family, and laughs accompany their strange immortality. The legacy they leave is often morbid, but first let me entertain you.

I called my mother the minute I heard about Fred MacMurray.

"I think I'll write about Uncle Sam from Poughkeepsie," I said.

"Sam from Poughkeepsie? That cheap bastard?" Mom said.

He's dead 40 years and that's how she remembers him.

He never had children, just plenty of whip-out. He'd show up in Passaic for the holidays laden with

Hershey bars for all us kids. My grandma named him General Hershey, and now my mother says to me, "Why would you want to write about General Hershey? He's liable to send you a bill."

When Fred MacMurray passed, my Rorschach read, after Sam from Poughkeepsie: Teddy Boss, Rudy Vallee, Cary Grant, Humphrey Bogart, Claude Rains, Walt Disney, Clark Gable, Harry Warren and J. Paul Getty.

You never heard of Teddy Boss? When a millionaire was a person with maybe $250,000, Teddy Boss was worth $20 million. He was from Passaic, however, so why would you hear of Teddy Boss? What you need to know about him now is that he got his hair cut every three weeks — at the Barbers College in Paterson.

Rudy Vallee needs no introduction. He was the pitcher on Frank Sinatra's El Cheapo All-Time All-Star baseball team. Rudy Vallee had more money than God and used to leave 10-cent pens with his name on them for tips. Ol' Blue Eyes, as big a spender as the world has seen, got a kick out of guys with tight elbows, and there's none of them he didn't know or know all about. The next time you drink with him, just ask him and you'll get the Hall of Fame.

Cary Grant was proud to be known as El Squeeko. When Cary's pajamas wore out, he'd order the pockets cut off to save the monograms. When he wanted to sell his house the broker told him to have it painted, that way was top dollar. Cary painted the front. "Nobody looks at the back," he said.

Humphrey Bogart grabbed the check from Paul Henreid at Rick's. It was the last check he ever picked up, if the people who drank with him at '21' and Chasen's have it right.

Claude Rains took the money from Rick and built a great summer house in Maine. Every afternoon he'd go to the country store to catch up on the latest paperback novels, priced 25 cents. He never bought one, he'd stand there reading until he worried about his heels running down and then he'd fold the page under until tomorrow.

Walt Disney clocked his cartoonists with a stopwatch on their way to the Coke machine. They got even the best they could by drawing porno sketches of Walt with Tinker Bell.

Clark Gable didn't give a damn. He'd make the greengrocers add up the bill four or five times before he'd pay the 60 cents.

Harry Warren wrote more hits than Irving Berlin, including *Plenty of Money and You*. He bitched until death that nobody ever asked him for his autograph, but he was the only guy in Hollywood who wouldn't hire a press agent. He once said, "I get physically ill when I have to pick up a check." When *42nd Street* became the biggest hit on Broadway, I asked him why he didn't come to New York to bask. He said: "The bastards won't send me a plane ticket."

J. Paul Getty, the world's richest man, put pay phones in his English palace. At his death, he was pricing pay toilets. Before his death his grandson was kidnapped. Mr. Getty refused to pay ransom. The kidnappers sent back the boy's ear, one of them. Even then, he hesitated. "I guess he's waiting to check the market on essential organs," somebody said. Eventually, the kid was ransomed and eventually the kid put himself away.

Propriety dictates against naming the living legends of parsimony, but don't worry about it, they're

flourishing out there. We have with us a hugely suc-
cessful Broadway songwriter of whom it is said he
"pulls his own teeth." The word on this guy is that
every time a waiter gets stiffed, he gets the royalties.

Then there is the great playwright who needs a
half-dozen computers to know how much money he
takes in daily. The only thing the computers close
down on is the word CHARITY.

A famous comedian who never stops talking about
his terrific investments, and all the dough that pours in
through the transom, went into a conniption fit the
day a new cleaning lady threw out the used soda bottles
he returns to the supermarket for the credit, natch.
Like I said above, however, you don't have to be rich
and famous or either or neither to make your way into
the parsimony pantheon.

All over the city there are women known as "hang
back wives" for the fact that in restaurants after their
husbands pay the check they have to figure out ruses
to hang back and throw a few extra bucks on the table
so that they can come back again without getting hair
in the soup.

The guys I love are those who invariably get an
irresistible yen for the cheapest item on the menu.
They always try to sell the rest of the table on it, if the
going is Dutch, because they worry that somebody
might say, "let's cut it four ways." Of course, they will
never go for that if theirs was a dime cheaper, but if
they can get the table to go lowballs, it's easier.

I've seen families destroyed over the objectively
inexplicable penuriousness of a father or mother, and
I'll bet everybody has seen something like it along the
way.

But you never hear of somebody saying to a person of that nature: "I think you have a problem. Why don't you seek help?"

To the contrary, cheap is generally considered "responsible." It's the big spenders ("profligates") who get the heat.

I wondered out loud the other day whether psychiatry is dealing with the situation. Dr. Harvey White, a well-known New York psychiatrist specializing in family therapy, was clearly relieved to be asked the question.

"It's a major problem, I deal with it at least twice a week," he said. "One of the big troubles is that it's in the psychiatric closet, so to speak. We don't address it as anything more than an individual quirk, if that. But penuriousness is a leading cause of family breakdown, probably on a par with alcoholism. And like alcoholism, it's a manifestation of something larger."

Explain, doctor.

"It's a defense against reality. It's a lack of faith in oneself. It's that old standby 'insecurity.' There's a fear that generosity will deprive the donor of love—you know, give a child too much and you'll lose his love. You're really afraid you'll lose his dependence, but you have to call it love. Under this umbrella, you keep your loved ones crippled. Then you wake up one morning and your grandson has a drug problem. And you have no idea why. But I see direct connections between penuriousness and such results, I see it all the time."

"Is there any psychiatric literature on the subject?"

"Practically nothing, it's virgin territory, which is amazing. We study everything about the human mind but this isn't even on our agenda."

"You think there ought to be a Cheapies Anonymous?" I ask.

"Good idea," Dr. White says. "But with an absolute rule. No donations allowed."

Which goes to show you. You can't even talk to a doctor about cheap guys without hearing shtick.

Did I tell you the one about Kate Smith?

# A Unit on *Guys and Dolls*

T his was going to be about the Middle East, but the Duke called and said we were on for *Guys and Dolls*. Well, nothing can keep me from *Guys and Dolls* unless it is Grace Kelly the way she looks in *Rear Window*, or maybe Audrey Hepburn the way she looks as *Sabrina*.

Of course, it is 15 years and change since anybody calls me to say we are on for *Guys and Dolls*. That was the first and until now the only Broadway revival of the show, but it didn't work, because they decided to gimmick it up with an all-black cast. This fit about as good as an all-white cast in *Raisin in the Sun*.

In the meantime, we have all had to make do with the movie, which won every Academy Award for miscasting. Frank Sinatra was perfect for Sky Masterson, but Marlon Brando was hot, so why should Samuel Goldwyn care if he couldn't sing? Sam Levene was the quintessential Nathan Detroit on stage, but Sinatra was pretty hot himself, so what could Goldwyn do but make him Nathan Detroit?

Of course, I watch it, anyway, as it is the only game in town, but you can imagine my excitement at the news that the show is on its way back to Broadway.

Indeed, I cannot wait for previews. I must get to the first rehearsal. And this is where the Duke enters.

His real name is John Hart, but even his mother calls him Duke, and surely everybody at the Yale Club bar and *shvitz*, which are the two places I run into him for maybe the last 10 years, when he is just out of college. He doesn't look like a Duke, exactly, but he doesn't look like a guy who has to work too hard for a living, either, and it turns out that what he does is to get citizens to put up their hard-earned potatoes so that the Duke and his associates can put shows up on the stage.

Now it is something of a long shot to suppose that Duke has a way of getting me into the first rehearsal of *Guys and Dolls*, or even the second rehearsal, because to arrange this he would have to have a piece of the action. In all the years I know him, Duke never has a piece of a sure thing, and if anything is a sure thing it is *Guys and Dolls* on Broadway.

But I am desperate, as I know the rehearsal is pending, it is any minute, and I am striking out, since it turns out that writers are not generally welcome at these events. So when I find myself sitting next to the Duke in the *shvitz*, which he calls the steam room, I say to him as follows: "Duke, do you happen to have an interest in *Guys and Dolls*?"

"Why, yes," he says. "I have a couple of units."

Now I know that a unit for *Guys and Dolls* runs north of a hundred grand, and while I always assume the Duke is comfortable, I never imagine he has the scratch to pick up one unit, forget about a deuce. Of course, it may be that Duke is involved with other people in this ownership, but that is none of my business.

"Duke," I say, "it is my opinion that weight for age, *Guys and Dolls* is the greatest musical of all time."

"Thank you," he says. "But I have never seen this show."

Well, he is a guy of thirtysomething, so this does not surprise me, and if it does surprise me I will not show it, for I do not wish to insult him at this time.

"Duke," I say, "do you think I could see the first rehearsal of this show?"

"Done," says the Duke.

Naturally, I do not get my hopes sky-high over this, for I hear show business types say "done" a thousand and one times, at the very least, and then I do not hear from them again. This is no disparagement of the Duke, who is, of course, sincere at all times, but if you ask me to lay two bobs on me showing up at the first rehearsal I will demand 4–1 and I will think I am giving away the best of it.

So there I am, three days later and nothing from the Duke, preparing my mind for an onslaught against George Bush and the State Department, I am ready to lay it in because here is an Administration pleasurably sticking it to Israel.

And that is when the phone rings and the Duke says: "We're on." He says: "It's 890 Broadway, 12:15."

I drop the Middle East, jump into the shower and my reverie begins.

My Uncle Abie had a book in West Philadelphia that provided him with fulsome whip-out throughout his life and never disturbed him with so much as a rap sheet, don't even think about jail.

The day I enrolled at the University of Pennsylvania, and just after my parents left me with tearful hugs and kisses, the first call I made was to Uncle Abie.

"How about a T-bone?" he said.

I met him at Bennie the Bum's, where I was received like I was Sinatra, and the first thing Abie did when he pushed the knife into the T-bone was to wave over the waiter.

"This is the hardest work I've done in 40 years," he said.

They delivered a new one on the spot and I delivered my marker a few months later when Abie showed in New York a night before the Friday night fights at the Garden.

I had picked up tickets for *Guys and Dolls* and somehow convinced my parents that I had to come home for the weekend and on a Thursday, no less.

Watching Abie watching *Guys and Dolls* was like watching Gary Cooper watching himself as Lou Gehrig. If Uncle Abie could sing, I lay 12–5 that Sam Levene gives him Nathan Detroit, in the interest of art.

When I arrive at the rehearsal, Peter Gallagher is singing beautiful, he is a wonderful Sky Masterson.

But I look at the Duke as for the first time and I see Sky as Damon Runyon saw Sky:

"He is maybe 30 years old, and is a tall guy with a round kisser, and big blue eyes, and he always looks as innocent as a little baby. But The Sky is by no means as innocent as he looks. In fact, The Sky is smarter than three Philadelphia lawyers, which makes him very smart, indeed."

The trouble is, the Duke cannot sing, and the further trouble is that the Duke needs a beard to cover up a chin that would be called glass were he to decide to challenge even a bantamweight in the ring.

Otherwise, he is Sky Masterson, my Uncle Abie would book it.

"Please, do not mention my chin," the Duke implores me.

But I do not feel obligated to him, for right at his side is a reporter from the *Hollywood Reporter*. I am told by the Duke that I have this rehearsal exclusive and here is Sydney Weinberg, girl reporter of the *Hollywood Reporter*.

"Are you related to the late Sidney Weinberg of Goldman, Sachs?" I ask.

"My grandfather," she says.

And now I am back in the Middle East.

Sidney Weinberg was a confidant of Franklin D. Roosevelt, a major money man for F.D.R. and a welcome visitor to the White House. One day he asked Roosevelt to do something about the murder of the Jews of Europe.

"I don't want you to talk about Jews to me," Roosevelt stopped him sharply. "Now or ever. I haven't time to listen to Jewish wailing."

Sidney Weinberg had never thought much about his Jewishness. But now he took the marble bust he had had made of F.D.R. and threw it from his penthouse window.

I asked his granddaughter if she had heard this story.

"You made my day," she said.

I got the horse right here.

# BROADWAY MY WAY

**W**hat are we doing calling *Guys and Dolls* a revival, are we crazy or something? Do we say we're going over to the Opera House to see a revival of *Rigoletto?* Or, hey, have you caught the revival of *Hamlet* at the Roundabout? Words count like money, honey, and they reveal a whole lot more. When we reduce a great American musical to "revival" we show an inferiority complex that would make Dr. Freud raise his eyebrows higher than a cat's back.

America can boast two unique contributions to art: jazz and the musical theater. So we pay our jazz greats off in uppercuts—there's not even a movie about Louis Armstrong, are you kidding?—and we dish off our great treasure trove of musicals as revivals that we're allowed to see about once every 25 years, if we're lucky, and then only when nothing else is working on Broadway. They're not even revivals if we can't see them again, and they are certainly not revivals to people who weren't born when *they* were born.

If *Guys and Dolls* had crapped out, we'd be reading a lot of stories today about how revivals don't work, how what we really need is a new American musical theater. Of course we need a new musical theater, and the hope is that *Guys and Dolls* will show the way.

The way is great melodies and always has been, and great lyrics to go with them, it should go without saying. You want to be singing or whistling the songs as you walk *out* of the theater, not when you're walking in, as in Andrew Lloyd Webber.

Maybe we have lost it, maybe something happened to the country, maybe we've lost our juice and our *joie*. No more melody runs through the minds of our songwriters? I don't believe it, and if I believed it I'd never admit it.

But we have lost our way, and for this I go after Stephen Sondheim, not for what he once was, but what he has become, and what his considerable influence has done to the songs we no longer can sing.

I recall a story he told years ago on Jonathan Schwartz's radio show. When he was a tyro lyricist, new to the scene, somebody brought together at a party a virtual hall of fame of songwriters to hear the kid do his stuff. Rodgers and Hammerstein were there, and Harold Arlen, and Yip Harburg and Burton Lane and Sammy Cahn and onward to Jule Styne. The only one who didn't cheer and holler was Jule Styne, according to young Mr. Sondheim.

"Naturally, he was the one I wanted to speak with," Mr. Sondheim said. "And Jule Styne said: 'You're afraid to swing for the fences, aren't you, kid?'"

He soon enough hit 'em over the fences—as a lyricist: *West Side Story*, music by Leonard Bernstein; *Gypsy*, music by Jule Styne.

When he wrote the music as well, he made some wonderful melodies. But I always thought that after he wrote *Anyone Can Whistle,* Stephen Sondheim decided that nobody would ever whistle to a Sondheim song again. I believe he set his sights on the Opera House, where once again — and who could blame him? — he was afraid to swing for the fences.

I don't say it was his intention, but in the event the American musical has suffered. So revered is Stephen Sondheim that most of the best songwriters followed him. Into the woods and without a song left for us to sing.

Not to suggest that the rock revolution had nothing to do with it, heaven forbid! It is no coincidence that the three last great American musicals — *Funny Girl, Hello Dolly!* and *Fiddler on the Roof* — came by on the very eve of the Beatles. Imagine telling Harold Arlen that he was history at age 55, and Jule Styne and all the rest of the great men who made this treasury. But that's exactly what they did, the money guys and dolls who were no longer producers but just on-the-make hustlers who had the chutzpah to tell us that we didn't want quality anymore.

The lines around the Martin Beck on the morning after the triumphant return of Nathan Detroit & Co. finally put the lie, in living color, to all of these philistines. The take was bigger than *Phantom of the Opera,* so take *that,* Andrew Lloyd, and take *that,* Mother England! Melody lives, and can the rest of the old haymakers be far behind?

*Annie Get Your Gun* opened Lincoln Center in 1966 and hasn't been heard from since in New York. Irving Berlin only wrote seven standards in that one. Cole Porter's best show, *Kiss Me, Kate,* hasn't been back since who knows when? How many kids have seen *Carousel?* Where is *Pal Joey,* for my money right up there with *Guys and Dolls? My Fair Lady* hasn't been here in 10 years, ditto *Oklahoma!* And how about *Finian's Rainbow,* last seen here in the mid-60's at the old City Center?

I asked Burton Lane about *Finian's* the day after *Guys and Dolls* broke up the town. He wrote the music and Yip Harburg the lyrics to this wondrous show. You want to hear some of the songs?

*How Are Things in Glocca Morra? If This Isn't Love. Old Devil Moon. Look to the Rainbow. When I'm Not Near the Girl I Love. That Great Come-And-Get-It Day. When the Idle Poor Become the Idle Rich.*

"How come the show hasn't been back in 25 years?" I asked Mr. Lane.

"We almost had it a couple of times," he said. "Beverly Sills was going to do it—twice!—at Lincoln Center. But both times she concluded that it was not politically correct."

What?

*Finian's Rainbow* was the first musical *against* racial prejudice.

"Right," said Mr. Lane. "But a white racist Senator is turned into a black man in the show. And this seems to have worried people, it was thought to be 'insensitive' to blacks. When we wrote it, in 1946, people worried that it was too pro-black, it was maybe insensitive to whites. Incredible, isn't it?"

Bet me. And bet me, too, that *Finian's Rainbow* will be back. Mr. Lane is in heavy discussions with a producer even as we speak. Those lines around the Martin Beck don't hurt, do they?

Money makes the world go 'round, the songwriter wrote. And never knock your own proposition, Mickey Cohen said.

So why am I so churlish?

This was, after all, an opening night like no other in at least 20 years in this town. Black-tie, glitter — not glitz, *glitter*. It lit up New York, *Guys and Dolls* did.

Coming on the heels of the Gershwins' *Crazy for You* and the very same Frank Loesser's *The Most Happy Fella*, why am I not *qvelling*?

Well, I am *qvelling*. But I want it to say something, I want it to give the message it deserves to those who write and those who finance. I want no more of this word "revival."

Maybe I can do it best by telling you how I really *qvelled* when my son, my about-to-be lawyer, called me from New Orleans the morning after *Guys and Dolls*.

"Dad," he said, "is it true? Am I finally going to be able to see *Guys and Dolls* on Broadway?"

\* \* \*

Stephen Sondheim sent me a blistering note re this column, accusing me of fabricating the anecdote about Jule Styne in order to "back up your point." Jule Styne, he wrote, wasn't at the party, nor were Rodgers and Hammerstein. Harold Arlen was there and it was Arlen who said something to him quite the opposite of my recollection: "You're afraid not to write a blockbuster, aren't you?"

I apologized to Sondheim for getting the story cockeyed, but I assured him that I wasn't trying to frame him.

"Believe it or not," I wrote, "I'm not quite so foolish as to make up a story in order to back up a point. You don't like the point, but look how easy it would have been to make it on the true facts: 'We are left to ponder what the musical theater would have been like today had Stephen Sondheim not taken Harold Arlen so literally.' "

Sondheim let it go at that, but I won't let Sondheim off the hook until he writes a song a guy and doll can whistle to instead of at.

# FEELING RUNYONESQUE

Ambrose Hammer, the late Shakespearean scholar and Broadway drama critic, wrote a review some fifty-odd years ago that stands the test of time, I think you will agree:

"After Mansfield Sothern's performance of *Hamlet* at the Todd Theater last night, there need no longer be controversy as to the authorship of the immortal drama. All we need do is examine the graves of Shakespeare and Bacon, and the one that has turned over is it."

If you have never heard of Ambrose Hammer and are in any event skeptical that anybody but Shakespeare or maybe Bacon could write such a great line and surely not a drama critic, you are chugging along pretty good at that. For there was no Ambrose Hammer, and of course no drama critic in history was capable of such a great line as evidenced by the fact that no drama critic in history ever wrote it.

On the other hand, Shakespeare didn't write it, nor did Bacon, and maybe a guy didn't have to be as smart as either of them to write it. Or maybe he did. Anyway, it is 20–1 and out that you did not know this great line was written by Damon Runyon, unless you are a Runyon scholar, although it is a probable 12–7 that you guessed it from the headline.

By now, anybody who has seen a road show of *Guys and Dolls,* not to mention the great new Broadway production, will know that I am in a Runyon frame of mind, what with some of these notes I am playing around with such as "20–1 and out," etc. Of course, there are plenty of citizens who believe I am always in a Runyon frame of mind, but these citizens do not know Runyon. Things being how they are these days, with smoke fascism on the wing and wine instead of gin, anybody who knows the way to Gallagher's bar and has the phone number of a bookmaker qualifies as "Runyonesque."

But Mickey Cohen told me long ago, "Never knock your own proposition," especially when it means a few potatoes for the damper, which is at present emptier than John Gotti's .45. The truth is, I have been a devotee of Alfred Damon Runyon since high school.

We used to play a game. What three things—a record, a movie, a book—would you take to a desert island?

I picked Louis and Ella, *Yankee Doodle Dandy,* and the stories of Damon Runyon.

I got no argument on Louis and Ella—these were the bright college years, before rock—and only a few raised eyebrows from *Casablanca* fans about *Yankee Doodle.* I love *Casablanca,* don't get me wrong, but all alone on a desert island I'd need a musical. When I said Runyon, I got the heat.

The received opinion in academia then was that Damon Runyon was fun, if you like that sort of thing, but be serious! You were supposed to get over that stuff in high school.

And this remains the received opinion. Bet me that Runyon is not on a single college reading list in the country. But I wouldn't take that bet, it would be grand larceny. Damon Runyon is out of print in the United States. In England, you can read him, they love him in sunny old England. But in America, no. Of course, our college professors never heard of Mickey Cohen, all we do here is knock our own proposition. How many years did it take for *Huckleberry Finn* to make the Harvard reading list?

Mark Twain would have seen Damon Runyon as his illegitimate son, and what other son would Mark Twain love? The Runyon tales, read front to back or vice versa, are the urban equivalent of *Huck Finn*, with Tom Sawyer as narrator.

As the guys and dolls at *The New York Review of Books* would say, permit me to explicate this thesis.

Runyon's people, from Big Jule the hit man to Nathan Detroit the entrepreneur of craps to the high roller Sky Masterson, are all doing the best they can, which is the best anybody can do if 9–5, not the odds but the hours, is what you will never do, God forbid.

They do not play hooky from school—what is school?—but from the System, and this of course is not just work, it is what comes from workaday, it is *why* you work. Which is to say dolls and what comes from dolls, which is to say children, which spells hostage if you are a guy who likes to get around and about and what good is a guy if he does not want to get around and about, just ask Huck Finn.

Pitfalls are everywhere, from the church to the law, but the only thing that can really get a guy under the thumb of the System is a doll. Love is the thing that can lick 'em, and Nathan Detroit was as much a victim as Antony.

Runyon has a story, "Barbecue," that I will put against Shakespeare anytime, and even against Genesis.

An old party named Greebins is stuffed into a bull-fiddle case by his young, ever-loving wife, Dimples, who wishes to bury him thus and use his money to support her busted-out lover, Juliano.

Saved by High-C Homer, and the Tom Sawyer narrator, who is always around and about, this old party Greebins refuses to confront Dimples, for she is "a nervous little thing," and he wishes only to get her back to home and hearth.

"Greebins," High-C Homer says, "do you mean to state that you will take her back after all this? Why?"

"I love her," Greebins says.

"Ah," Homer says. "I see your point."

And the professors choose Hemingway?

I got the horse right here.

# III

## SEX, DRUGS, LIES AND LAWS

# SOL WACHTLER
# AS GODFATHER

Insiders are saying something altogether different about Sol Wachtler and why he did what he did to Joy Silverman, his ex-mistress. The conventional wisdom is that there is no wisdom, no rational explanation for the former Chief Judge's wild fear campaign against Ms. Silverman that resulted in his spectacular arrest and dramatic downfall. Everybody, it seems, has been searching for new ways to spell "bizarre."

But quietly, and ever so anonymously, a relatively rational explanation for his behavior has been emerging among a few judges and lawyers who have known Sol Wachtler for many years. It goes something like this.

After Ms. Silverman left his bed for the New Jersey lawyer David Samson, Judge Wachtler became obsessed with getting her back. And so devised what he considered a brilliant, foolproof method of getting her attention—and getting her to rush to him for help.

Thus the campaign of terror—the phone calls, the letters, the threat to kidnap the daughter, the demand for money—ever escalating as Ms. Silverman continued to ignore him. He figured she'd run to him quickly, if not immediately. It made sense: He's always had a complex relationship with her that must have included the "father thing," as the late George Bush would say. But here weeks were going by, the threats jumping to fail-safe limits, and no call for help came from Joy.

Of course, what he didn't figure on was that she'd go to the director of the F.B.I. Perhaps he should have considered the possibility, given Ms. Silverman's access to the White House, but even if he did, who could ever factor in William Sessions' response? You don't have to be crazy or even obsessed to laugh off the notion that the F.B.I. would put half the Bureau on an anonymous caller, no matter how much juice the callee had with the President. I mean, John Gotti was treated like a petty larceny thief next to what the Bureau laid on here.

It is said that when Ms. Silverman was told that her caller was none other than Judge Wachtler, she tried to call the whole thing off. But alas, it was now out of her hands, and how she must have understood then and there—she is nothing if not worldly—that this thing would harm her as much as it would do in Sol.

Indeed, there are those who wonder who was more shocked—Judge Wachtler when he was pulled over by the Feds on the Long Island Expressway, or Joy Silverman when she discovered the identity of her tormenter.

The pinch, recall, was on the day that Sol Wachtler was to have picked up the 20-grand ransom. And here he was getting picked up by the F.B.I. Could anyone have thought that he was serious about ransom, once they knew who he was? But what was the F.B.I. to think; it's not theirs to wonder why, only to make the bust.

Look how wonderful the Wachtler strategy was, and you may begin to understand his surprise at the way it all ended. Joy Silverman would run to him and he would assure her that he'd use all of his powers to remove the threat to her, to her new lover, to her child. Sol Wachtler as Godfather! Perfect.

One can only imagine how beautiful it would be the day Sol Wachtler was able to tell Joy Silverman that nobody would bother her again.

People who knew him well, and others who saw him in action during the time of his ultimate caper, have remarked on how normal he was, how he performed his tasks per usual, brilliantly. Not simply on the bench, but in all those thankless chores he took on as Chief Judge of the New York Court of Appeals. Do you know what it means to speak at these bar association dinners in Onondaga County, in Hudson?

The boredom level alone would be too much for the average man, forget the witty and bright jurist. But Sol Wachtler thrived on all of this, and it didn't bother him a whit that the next call he was about to make was a crazed threat to his old girlfriend.

Why? Because it was the smartest way he knew to get her to come crawling back. And how could it hurt him, who would ever dream that Sol Wachtler was up to such madness?

It's only a theory, sure, this scenario writ now by the insiders. But I think it beats the conventional wisdom, and the story about the brain tumor, by a healthy 20-1.

However, it's 100-1 and out that this will not be Sol Wachtler's defense in the criminal court. Just a caper? If he says that, he goes to jail. Faced with the Federal guidelines, a sentencing judge would be forced to imprison him for a set term—unless he can prove insanity, in at least one of its legally approved forms. If all you did you did to get the girl back, that ain't insanity in a courtroom, baby.

And maybe it's not insanity at all. The feminists would never think so, certainly not, but what do they know about the fury of a man scorned? Except that he'd better go to the can.

It is irony at its height. If the insiders are correct, Sol Wachtler belongs at home, not in prison. But he can only avoid *durance vile* by saying he didn't know what he was doing.

Of course, all of forensic psychiatry is irony. You don't go to jail if you're crazy, only if you're sane. We want meshuggenahs on the street and sane people in the slammer?

Sol Wachtler was a great judge, I heartily join the conventional wise men and women on that point. But there is a funny aspect to his tragedy.

If the insiders have it right, if he wanted to play godfather to Joy Silverman, consider what the mafiosi would think of his apparent desire for continued house arrest.

What Mafia man would choose house arrest over prison? The answer is, none. In *any* given situation, no real wiseguy would stand still for such a horrific sentence. Hell, we could ruin organized crime in America by refusing to put these guys in the can, by insisting that they spend the rest of their lives with their wives. They would take deportation over that, they'd take that plus ratting out the entire social club if they had to face life with the old lady.

And that's for killing somebody or breaking a few

knees. Imagine what they'd do if you had them on a mistress deal? The chair is preferable, don't even argue the point.

So here is Sol Wachtler's lawyer, trying to get him home for what otherwise would be a comfortable five spot, say, in one of those kibbutz joints.

If it happens, and the odds are it will happen that way, watch the feminists go to it on the Op-Ed pages.

While John Gotti, in solitary, laughs.

# WILLIAM KENNEDY SMITH AND TRIAL BY HEADLINES

ꟼꟼꟼ

It happened that William Kennedy Smith received his freedom during Freedom Week, a few days before the 200th anniversary of the Bill of Rights. As it also happened, his jury acquitted him a couple of hours before the Columbia Journalism School celebrated the birth of the First Amendment.

Mr. Smith could thank certain parts of the Bill of Rights, such as the right to counsel and trial by jury, but the First Amendment didn't fare too well, no good at all. If left to the power of the press, Willie Smith would have only the freedom of bail today while looking at 15 years in the slammer.

So many defendants have been scorched with trial by headline across the years that it would be presumptuous to say one never saw anything like what the press did to William Kennedy Smith. What makes this one unique, however, is the nature of the charge itself.

Date rape, unlike other crimes, is not a question of whodunit but whether it was done at all. In the rare case, perhaps, there can be little doubt, as when the woman is beaten and the body shows it. But as a rule, no, and so the only issue is, was there a crime committed?

And that is the way it was here: The only bodily harm alleged by Patricia Bowman was a bruised rib, which hardly classified her as the Central Park jogger.

Yet she was practically treated as such by the news media, which with rare exceptions protected her name, her face and her reputation. The reason given is that rape stigmatizes a woman and if the press does not commit self-censorship, other victims will be discouraged from pressing charges against their date rapists.

You can throw "alleged" into the formulation day in and day out, without losing what you set out to do: convince the reader that the woman has been raped, because the woman says she has been raped.

Every criminal lawyer knows that the most difficult thing to do in a rape case is to get the jury thinking about the presumption of innocence. Why would any woman charge rape, with all the ignominy involved, if it were not true?

When the press then refuses to so much as name her, it not only reinforces this notion, it turns the presumption of innocence on its head. So infamous is this crime, they say, we will not further harm this poor woman by revealing her identity!

It is one thing to do this for the Central Park jogger, where there was no question that the crime was committed, she was practically ruined, why make it worse for her? When you do the same for the "alleged victim" of Mr. Smith, you are prejudging the only issue in the case: Was there a rape?

I happen not to agree that a woman raped is a woman stigmatized. And I venture to say that few people in the media believe it. The only stigma is on the rapist, where it ought to be. It wasn't that way 30 years ago or even 20, when cops and prosecutors often dismissed complainants as sluts and treated them as if they were the perpetrators.

But a sea change came over the law beginning in the mid-70's, as one state after another threw out requirements of corroboration and even the "fresh outcry" rule, which required that a woman make her charge soon after the violation. It is today the case in many jurisdictions that a man can be indicted for rape on the uncorroborated statement of a woman made long after the alleged incident.

Moreover, those district attorneys have special rape units, and these units are more often than not staffed by women.

These revolutionary changes, not always consistent with civil liberty, were generally welcomed by Americans, who quite understood, men and women alike, that the enforcement authorities had too long treated rape with cavalier contempt for the victims.

None of this could have happened, I suggest, if the old nonsense about stigmatism had prevailed. To the contrary. The major thing that fuels the myth is the patronizing notion that we dare not say the name of the woman.

I am hardly alone here; important elements of the feminist movement have said the same, or close. But even if I'm wrong, say I'm dead wrong, say a woman coming forward with a rape charge stands to lose her reputation forever, does this dispose of the issue?

Well, there happen to be other values involved, such as the First Amendment, such as the rights of the accused in criminal prosecutions.

If the Government ordered the press to withhold

the name of an accuser, how many minutes do you think it would take for it to be challenged? And how many seconds before any judge worth his oath would gavel down the bureaucratic hand that would dare censor the free press?

And yet here self-censorship is not only condoned, it is applauded. Self-censorship is the dirty little secret of American journalism—every copy boy knows that—but here it is proud, out in the open and prancing as if Thomas Jefferson were saying, yes, indeed.

We have lost our way when we decide that the role of the press is to protect not the accused but the accuser.

William Kennedy Smith was raked over by the news media, and that is freedom of the press, and no government has the right to stop it, and I would have it no other way. But don't tell us that this is the obligation of the press while you make the accuser sacrosanct.

Florida law protects a rape accuser from revelations about her background. Mr. Smith's lawyers were forbidden from cross-examining her regarding her past. When *The New York Times* ran a story about certain aspects of her life, and named her in the bargain, Max Frankel was put on the stand by hundreds of members of his staff, as if *he* were the Central Park rapist. Nobody complained about naming Willie Smith. Patricia Bowman, however, later became anonymous again in the Gray Lady.

Now we read that Mr. Smith's acquittal does not mean innocence, it's just that the jury could not find guilt beyond a reasonable doubt. Thus sayeth *Newsday* editorially, and Sidney Schanberg, and a variety of columnists who can hardly hold back their bitterness that this bastard has gone free. In *The New York Post*, the estimable Amy Pagnozzi wrote, Don't worry, Willie Smith will be back, he'll do it again.

The only verdict an American jury can deliver other than guilty is not guilty. To insist on a verdict of innocent is to insist that a defendant prove the negative.

And now we hear complaints that the judge didn't allow into evidence statements by three other women who claimed that years earlier William Kennedy Smith did or tried to rape them on dates. Moira Lasch, the fabulous prosecutor, filed these depositions in court and thus got around the gag rule and got it in the papers.

It's called "pattern crimes," and the law is strict on its admissibility for the best of reasons. We are supposed to try people for the crime indicted, not for previous allegations. The only time this stuff is allowed in evidence is when it amounts to fingerprints—it has to be virtually that close in pattern to what is now charged. This is called America.

And how American is it to run these stories by faceless, nameless accusers?

It is, I suppose, politically correct. The next time I hear that phrase I reach for my revolver. And if you care about the Bill of Rights, cover me.

# ANITA HILL AND UNCLE TOM

W hy did Anita Hill turn down the chance to confront her accusers on the Senate Judiciary Committee? Why didn't she come back that Sunday morning and put the cat to the Messrs. Hatch, Simpson and Specter? Why hasn't anybody in the media asked that question when they seem to have asked every other question?

In my opinion, her decision to walk away from the fray, just when she was delivered the high ground by her hit men, cinched the nomination for Clarence Thomas. Had she showed up instead of taking a powder, she would have put away these neo-McCarthyite opponents for fair and buried Clarence Thomas in the bargain.

She was, after all, a great witness. She was the best witness I ever saw, and I've seen my elegant sufficiency. Nobody understood this better than George Bush. His minions went to the whip because they knew Clarence Thomas could not save himself. Clarence Thomas could have cried a river and nobody, including the supine, collusive Democratic majority, could have brought him back to life after Anita Hill. All

that was left was an assault on the character of Anita
Hill.

They didn't do it to her face. Orrin Hatch was
almost sweet-toothing her, and Alan Simpson laid nary
a glove on her. Arlen Specter, the chief gun, did not
accuse her of perjury until the day *after* she testified.
Please don't talk about me when I'm gone, goes the old
song, and these guys turned it on its head.

Politics ain't beanbag, right? Anita Hill, for whatever reason, came forward against Clarence Thomas,
and once she did that she had to understand that
everything else goes.

What I don't get is why she walked away just when
she could have whacked out all of her accusers, Arlen
Specter included.

I mean, if Arlen Specter really believed she committed perjury "flat out," then he ought to go back to
the record and ask for pardons for those people he put
away on the inconsistent statements of witnesses while
he was the District Attorney of Philadelphia. The
prisons are loaded with inmates, particularly mafiosi,
who wouldn't be there except for the uncorroborated,
inconsistent testimony of accomplices, who got a walk
because they gave up guys the government wanted.

But that is as nothing next to what Anita Hill
could have done to Orrin Hatch and Alan Simpson.

Senator Hatch accused her of fabricating her testimony out of a well-known novel and an obscure law
case. In *The Exorcist*, somebody wants to know who
put the pubic hair in his gin. The law case speaks of an
"elongated penis." Q.E.D., said Orrin Hatch, that's
where Anita Hill got the lines she attributed to
Clarence Thomas. Imagine what Anita Hill could have

done to him with those great reaches. I'm telling you, Mr. Hatch would have been looking under the nearest rug for the escape.

Senator Simpson, Wyoming's answer to Gary Cooper, the big cowboy who held up his file as if to say "I have here in my hands . . ." and talked about his evidence of Anita Hill's "proclivities"—if she had put it to him to prove it, where do you think Alan Simpson would be today?

I don't know about you, but I never missed Joseph Welch so much as right then and there. Joseph Welch, the Boston lawyer who discomfited Joseph McCarthy in the Army-McCarthy hearings when McCarthy accused one of his law associates of a flirtation with communism. "Let us not assassinate this lad further, Senator," Mr. Welch said. "You have done enough. Have you no sense of decency, sir, at long last? Have you left no sense of decency?"

To be sure, Anita Hill had nobody like Joseph Welch in her corner, but she had herself, which was plenty good enough for her first round and would have only improved the second time around.

Of course, even as I write I can hear her backers getting their backs up. In some quarters, no criticism of Anita Hill will be countenanced. She did a great service, she was pilloried by these men, who could suggest that she come back and subject herself to more of this disgraceful business?

The answer is, you don't lay down your arms until the war is over. Anita Hill was out there making charges that if believed would have kept Clarence Thomas off the Supreme Court. When the Republican senators went after her character, she owed it to herself—and I suggest she owed it to her supporters around the country—to come back in and give 'em hell. And then she would have won, I say again. Really, with what she was going to do, it would have been batting practice, my mouth was watering what she was going to do to the firm of Hatch, Simpson & Specter.

Of course, the fundamental tragedy is that Clarence Thomas was on his feet when Ms. Hill came forward. On his feet? He had a locked-up 54 votes and more to come. All of his quite formidable opposition was deflated, including the feminists.

In the wake of the final vote, the feminists have vowed to take it out on those Democrats who provided the winning margin for Mr. Thomas. But where were they before the Hill allegations surfaced? Sure they were against him, but let's face it, there was no heat.

Why did it take sexual harassment charges to actuate the opposition? Of course such charges are serious, but they pale next to the statist views of Clarence Thomas. And I submit that they pale next to what he did to his sister, which never came up in the hearings, and I'll never understand that, either.

Mr. Thomas once said about her: "She gets mad when the mailman is late with her welfare check. That's how dependent she is. What's worse is that now her kids feel entitled to the check, too. They have no motivation for doing better or getting out of that situation."

The real story, as reported by *The Los Angeles Times* on July 5, was that the sister, Emma Mae Martin, went on welfare to care for an aunt who suffered a stroke. Before that, and while Mr. Thomas was in Yale Law School, Emma Mae Martin, a deserted wife, supported her three children with minimum-wage jobs. After her aunt passed, Ms. Martin went back to work, and her kids now have jobs or are in school.

Even if none of this were true, what kind of man trashes his sister in public? And yet the White House demands confirmation on the grounds of character. O.K., the word was, if you don't think he's a Louis Brandeis, you've got to admit he's the American Dream.

Now that he's in, a new dream has surfaced. It is said that having suffered the arrows of Ms. Hill, Clarence Thomas will be sensitive to the rights of criminal defendants and to the right of privacy.

Maybe. But only if he was innocent. If he did what Anita Hill says he did, the lesson he's likely to learn is how easy it is to beat the rap.

# UNCLE NUNCHICK
# AND THE FLOOZIE

I learned sexual harassment as a child at the feet of the women I knew most intimately: my Aunt Geshka, my grandmother, the maid Anna and, yes, my mother.

It began at my first funeral. I was 6 years old. It was for a great-aunt. I don't remember her name, nor her husband's, but the scene I remember like it was yesterday.

The great-uncle was dying to jump into the grave after his wife. My uncles and cousins were holding him back like crazy.

Aunt Geshka said, "Let go of him." The uncles and cousins said, "Are you nuts? He's going to jump into the grave!"

"Let go of him!" Geshka said, and they let go of him. He fell backwards.

Geshka turned to me and said: "Let that be a lesson to you, kid."

As we left the funeral grounds, the great-uncle cried out: "I walk alone!" Aunt Geshka directed my attention to a blond 20 feet behind him and said: "He won't walk alone for long."

Three months later they were married. Because they didn't wait the 11-month mourning period, we all boycotted the wedding. Except Geshka, who reasoned that somebody had to be there to report back to the family. Geshka was better than Walter Winchell, are you kidding? "He dressed her in mink, whaddaya think?" Geshka said. My grandma nodded sagely. "How did he meet her?" my mother asked. "Whaddaya think?" Geshka said. "She was the secretary, she can't even type."

When I was 10, my Uncle Nunchick had a stroke. My mother and my grandmother took me to Brooklyn to see him. He didn't look too hot, his face was curved out left and his nose the other way and with a drip. His wife, my Aunt Yetta, looked worse, the way she was scowling at poor Nunchick. She said: "Where is she now, Nunchick?"

I had no idea, but I saw my mom and my grandma tighten up.

"Where is she *now*, Nunchick?" Yetta said it again.

"Leave him alone," my grandma said.

"He left me alone 15 years, I should leave him alone now?"

Nunchick seemed to be smiling just a tad. And she caught it, I think. She got right into his messed-up face and real loud she said: "Where is she *now*, Nunchick, where are the sables you wrapped her in, where are the diamonds, *where*, Nunchick, where?"

Nunchick raised himself up somehow and with great dignity he said: "She had class, Yetta, *class*."

These were his last recorded words. Oy, did Aunt Yetta give it to him then.

Ten days later we were at Nunchick's funeral and I mortified my mother and grandmother by asking Yetta, where is she now? I said, is she here, Aunt

Yetta? Geshka had put me up to it and Geshka started to clap when Yetta said: "I was afraid to ask her. If she shows up anywhere near him they won't be able to close the coffin."

The maid Anna was a spinster and this bothered my mother, my grandmother and Geshka, once they got to like her and had taught her to speak the Queen's Yiddish. Thursday was Anna's night off and Geshka started taking her to the bingo in Wallington. She figured this was a way for Anna to meet somebody eligible, and one night, sure enough, they found Johnny.

From then on, Johnny showed at our house every Thursday, and my Aunt Sara, known as "Kid Sara," played "Oh Johnny" on the piano while Johnny tapped his feet. "Oh Johnny, Oh Johnny, how you can love." Then we cleared out to the movies, leaving the maid Anna to harass Johnny all alone. A week after France fell to Hitler, Johnny fell to Anna and my grandmother paid for the wedding.

I didn't think of it that way at the time, but obviously what I have recalled here were instances of sexual harassment in the workplace. Years later I saw the same sort of thing play out in saloons, but first let me tell you what Aunt Geshka told me the night I graduated high school.

Here are the facts of life, she told me: "Never marry for love, it flies out the window. Marry a girl so rich that when you wake up in the morning you sing to her, 'I'll Get By as Long as I Have You.'" She downed a shot of schnaps and I figured I was dismissed. "Wait a minute, where you going?" Geshka said. "Don't be in a hurry. I want you to learn something. And here it is: No old poor guy ever married a beautiful young woman."

Well, I did not listen to Geshka on the rich girl. Out of some perverse rebellion I married a girl I loved with a dowry that consisted entirely of a lease I had to use a sky marker to get her out from under. I guess I hoped one day she'd sing "I'll Get By" to me, but it's going on 30 years now and no dice.

On the other hand, I had a truly perverse desire to prove Geshka wrong about poor old guys never hooking up with beautiful young women. In search of just one like that, I started going to saloons eastside, westside, uptown, downtown.

I still do it, I'm still on the prowl, but I confess I never did hear tell of an old poor guy getting it on with a beautiful young woman. But in my search I found out much about sexual harassment that I would like to share with the reader.

The Lion's Head is in Greenwich Village and has been there 25 years come later this month. Nothing ever changes in the Lion's Head other than guys losing it and dropping on the wagon. I go back to its start, when I was a tyro newspaperman with nothing better to do than waste my youth singing songs in good saloons.

Which is what we would do, us guys, sing Jolson songs and the Mills Brothers right up until last call. But always a woman would show up, just as it was getting mellow, a woman would sidle to a guy saying, "Honey, let's go, c'mon, it's late, let's go home."

These were never wives and sometimes not even girlfriends or mistresses. The poor guy would want one more for the road but these women were persistent and very rough indeed. The guy would finally collapse and leave with her, looking back at us with that funny grin that spells nothing else but sexual harassment.

Some years ago, I was drinking with Murray the Millionaire and his mistress Fayzie in the little bar back of Frankie & Johnnie's on the second floor at 45th and Eighth. Fayzie decided to use the facility and so was gone when the phone rang and Cappy the bartender turned to Murray the Millionaire and said, "Are you here?"

Naturally, Murray said he was not here, but whoever was on the line was not taking this for an answer, and finally Cappy motioned to Murray that he better be there.

Right away, Murray the Millionaire's face turned white and he handed me a couple of hundred and said as follows: "Myra's downstairs in the phone booth and she's coming up here to nail me. I'll get her out, you take care of Fayzie and tell her anything but the truth."

The phone booth was right outside the door leading up to the bar, and as Murray ran down I looked down and sure enough there was his wife Myra coming up the stairs. It was a heartrending scene, what with Murray pushing down and Myra pushing up and in all my travels before and since I have never seen a man fight off sexual harassment as courageously as the great Murray the Millionaire.

But now I had the problem, because Fayzie figured this out in no time flat and of course all she wanted was to get me in bed to get even with Murray. Fayzie was a great-looking woman with black eyes and killer thighs and I had all I could do to fend her off. Naturally it helped that Murray the Millionaire was not beyond getting a wiseguy to break a couple of my legs and maybe the third, and I was sure that Fayzie would tell him, since why else do it, so I don't give myself points for courage.

Speaking of wiseguys, they are easily the most sexually harassed species on earth. Wiseguys are more terrified of going home to their old ladies than having an open contract out on their lives. Often they are afraid of their girlfriends as well, which is why on the whole they prefer jail to the streets. That way they never have to go home and no heat from the girlfriends either and they get their sex sent in and without harassment.

But you don't have to be a wiseguy to suffer under constant sexual harassment, and I thought I would bring this to your attention since my brothers, wise or regular guys, are always afraid to say anything about this and so live with the condition in hellish silence.

# How To Save
# Roe vs. Wade

❏❏❏

When Stanley Woodward returned to the sports pages of his beloved *New York Herald-Tribune* in 1959, after 11 years of forced exile, he led off his first column with these words: "As I was saying, before I was so rudely interrupted . . ."

What brings that old beauty back to my room is a call I got from the editor of this newspaper reminding me that I was present at the creation, that I committed a column on Robert Bork and the Supreme Court for Vol. 1, No. 1 of the beloved Observer.

My *interruptus* was of the coitus variety, induced by circumstances too boring to relate. It was the first time I wasn't fired from a column, and unless I get out of this lead soon it won't be the last time. You should know, however, that mine editor suggested that I somehow note the historic roots of my return to these pages, and I sure as hell wasn't going to do that without Stanley Woodward's protection.

On the other hand, as I was saying when Mr. Bork was so rudely interrupted by the Senate on his way to the Supreme Court, his rejection, however welcome, was hardly likely to change the direction of the Court, even on the cutting-edge issues surrounding *Roe v. Wade*.

That was an easy call, to say the least, despite the fact that advocates on either side of the Bork nomination spoke and acted as if the sky would fall depending on which way the Senate voted. And it was easy despite the fact that the Senate for the first time in living memory fulfilled its Constitutional obligation to provide "advice and consent," by closely questioning a nominee's views of the Great Charter and not just looking into whether he smoked marijuana in college or joined a discriminatory club or turned a few dubious bucks once upon a time.

What was clear, even as the Senators at Mr. Bork's hearing gloried in their devotion to privacy, to women's rights, to the Bill of Rights, was that this was an exercise brought on more by the candidate's paper trail, not to say his contentious persona, than by their own collective view of their responsibility and power to protect the Constitution. You knew damn well that the next guy was going to walk right in. And you didn't have to wait for the next guy, you just had to remember the way they unanimously confirmed the last guy, Antonin Scalia.

In the event, as all in the Republic know, we got Anthony Kennedy for Robert Bork and then we got David Souter for William J. Brennan Jr. And on May 23 we got *Rust v. Sullivan*. Four years after the great debate on Robert Bork, a 5–4 Court ruled that Federally financed family planning clinics cannot advise women of their rights to abortion under *Roe v. Wade*.

Egregious as the result is, it pales before the activism and cold-blooded statist judicial philosophy that fueled it. The clinics have been giving abortion advice for nearly two decades, with Congress continuing to pay the bill. That Reaganite bureaucrats wrote a regulation banning it in 1988 was accepted by most people for what it was: an ideological arrogation of power by the executive branch. Regulations must follow the will and intent of the statute. That is black-letter law if there ever was black-letter law.

To uphold that regulation, then, the Court had to find that there was no contrary Congressional intent and that the regulation did not violate the free-speech clause of the First Amendment. But what self-respecting strict constructionist would get to the Constitutional argument when the case was so obviously disposable by reference to Congressional intent? That was Sandra Day O'Connor's position in dissent, and she was upholding as old and venerable a doctrine as there is in Constitutional law.

But Justices William Rehnquist, Byron White, Scalia, Kennedy and Souter were not going to allow a little thing like judicial conservatism to get in the way of their own conservative political agenda. That, of course, is exactly what the Right always accused the Warren Court of doing, "making law," but for some 20 years now nobody's done it better than these Supreme Court darlings of the Right.

They have gotten away with it by cloaking themselves in the mantle of judicial self-restraint, but the only thing they have managed to restrain is their own laughter. Ever since the Warren Court's demise—circa 1971—the Supreme Court has systematically eviscerated the Bill of Rights. Because most of the victims were criminal defendants, however, the only sound we heard from the press was applause. The liberals didn't even give the sound of one hand up in a stop sign. Indeed, the liberal law school professors promoted the incredible line that the Court had not changed significantly under Warren Burger.

Alas, there was no H.L. Mencken around to straighten things out. In the 1920's, the Sage of Baltimore noted that the only part of the Bill of Rights that had not been violated by the Supreme Court was the Third Amendment's proscription against quartering troops in peacetime. Give this Rehnquist Court a few more years and a couple of more "strict constructionists," and don't be surprised if you find a few stormers in the living room.

There is always hope, and I'm here to provide silver linings. It could be that the Court inflicted a wound on its heartless soul with this decision. Until now, as I just said, the people who suffered most from its rulings were the criminals. And criminals have no constituency. What was needed all these years was an activist group who could make themselves heard for the Constitution, who could at least get a debate going in the land.

The pro-choice lobby is anything but quiet, bless them, and they would bless us all and help themselves if they turned this decision into a broad-scale assault on the judicial statists who are destroying our great Constitution day in, day out. After all, if the Bork affair proved anything, it was that single-issue politics can serve only as a temporary palliative. In the event, the only thing the Administration had to do to put another statist on the Court in Mr. Bork's place was to find someone without a paper trail. The Senators fell all over themselves in praise of Anthony Kennedy and practically stood mute in front of David Souter, who seemed never to have written anything.

But both Mr. Kennedy and Mr. Souter had records on the core liberties protected by the Bill of Rights, and these records left no doubt as to where they'd stand. So far they have not disappointed—almost invariably they stand with the Government. As does most of this Court. The close vote in *Rust v. Sullivan* was the only real surprise the decision had to offer.

Can *Roe v. Wade* be far behind?

What I'm trying to say here in my dopey fashion is that the best and perhaps only way to save *Roe* is to try to save what's left of our Bill of Rights.

It's all connected, and if we don't get it, there'll be no bones left to pick.

# BLACKMAILERS AND AIDS

□□□

W hen he slipped the paper under my pen, the doc, I was about to fix the old John Doe on without a look, what the hell this was only an insurance exam, but my left eye caught the top of the page and the pen froze in my hand.

"Didn't they tell you about this?" the doc said.

"Nothing."

"They're supposed to inform you."

"Does that mean I have a choice?"

"Only if you don't want the policy," the doc said.

So there I was, face to face with mandatory testing for the AIDS virus.

"Does everybody get this funny look when you hit 'em with this?" I asked, as I signed on the dotted line.

"Especially doctors," he said. "Always sticking pins in people, you know."

"Oh, when do I find out?"

"Takes about a week. We send it to a lab in Kansas."

"So you'll call me when you know."

"Only if there's a problem. The company will call."

"Well, uh, I'll be away all next week, just my answering machine. If the company leaves a message it means I'm positive?"

"Not necessarily," the doc said. "Sometimes the vial breaks in transit. Then the postal authorities throw it away, they won't handle it. So the call might only mean we have to do the test again."

"But if it's negative, they don't bother to tell me?"

"Sure. You'll get the policy. That's the way you'll know."

"How long does that take?"

"About the same time, a week, maybe a couple days more."

It occurs to me that maybe I am giving this doctor the idea that I am worried, when naturally I am not worried at all, what is there to worry about?

I chuckle. I always chuckle when I'm not worried.

"This will be an interesting medical experiment," I say.

"Why so?" the doc says.

"Because if I'm HIV-positive, it means you can get it from a toilet seat."

Now the doc chuckles and proceeds to take my blood pressure.

"Don't you think you should have done this before you gave me the AIDS test?"

"Very good," he says. "Very fine pressure."

The minute the doc leaves—I didn't tell you this was a house call because I didn't want to lose my credibility—I go into the bedroom to inform my wife of my fine blood pressure. It is 7:30 A.M.

"My blood pressure is 140 over 80," I say. "And my heart is good."

"How nice," she says, turning over and grabbing the pillow.

"He gave me the AIDS test."

There is a silent moment.

Then: "What for?"

I notice she is sitting upright.

"You set up the appointment. Didn't they tell you?"

"Nothing," she says.

I chuckle.

"Go back to sleep, honey," I say.

The reason for this physical examination is as pure 1980's as AIDS. The insurance company that covered me for 25 years went bankrupt. So I was assigned a new carrier and they demanded a new physical.

Nothing mandatory about an AIDS test under these circumstances. Like the doc said, "Only if you don't want the policy."

He said it like Marcus Welby but the message was out of Roy Cohn: No mail travels faster than blackmail.

Without blackmail I would never have agreed to be tested.

But if anybody told me that, I would have taken him outside.

What did I have to fear?

I'm not a homosexual, I'm not a drug addict. I have never had a blood transfusion.

And yet the pen froze in my hand. I had to ask myself, why?

On the surface, the answer could have been Roy Cohn. In 1985, Random House asked me to help him write his autobiography. It was a funny choice in some ways—I had nothing in common with his politics, to say the least. But I had known him for 20 years and in a crazy way I liked him. And he trusted me.

But he was full-blown AIDS. I would be spending months with him. At that time very little was known about how one could contract the virus. I called the best AIDS doctors in the world and was told, unequivocally, not to worry.

One doctor was contrary. "The state of the art on AIDS," he said, "is that there is no state of the art. If you ask me, I would stay away."

I wrote the book with Mr. Cohn and in the ensuing seven years, thought no more of it.

And then thought of little else in the week I waited for HIV-negative.

Of little else, but not of nothing else.

The truth, I started to get it, was that I would have been worried anyway.

Why, after all, had I not been tested if I was really worried about Roy Cohn?

Only when the insurance policy came through, when I knew for sure that I was HIV-negative, did I understand why I would never have volunteered to be tested, why it took blackmail.

Even then, I only got the answer through what the law schools call the Socratic Method.

It is right after the Knicks beat the Bulls in Game Four, we are talking Sunday night, May 10, the place is Gallagher's bar, 52nd and Broadway. This crowd I know for years, the crowd is such that not one of them believes that Magic Johnson got it from a woman. Nathan Detroit is politically correct next to the guys I am drinking with at Gallagher's, just so you get the idea.

"Has anybody here been tested for AIDS?" I ask.

The martinis freeze in their hands. I get more shaking heads than a rock band.

Finally, the one lawyer among them comes to and says: "Why, did you?"

"Certainly."

"And?"

"Negative. I tested out negative."

They all say "terrific," but there is envy in their eyes.

"Why did you do it?" the lawyer says.

"The question is, why didn't *you* do it?" I say.

"I don't know," he says.

"Well," I say, "is it not true that it can take several years before an HIV-positive becomes full-blown AIDS?"

"Yes."

"That's the answer."

"What's the answer?"

"If you test positive, you lose the years you have, it becomes every waking moment. And that seems to be strong enough to cancel out your obligation to others, and even your own self-interest, because it now looks like early discovery can prolong your life."

"Let's talk about the Knicks," the lawyer said, and the smiles came back to the bar at Gallagher's.

# MEANWHILE,
# ENGLAND SLEEPS

"**H**ow is the drug problem in your country?"
Paul O'Dwyer, the New York reformer, asked the visiting chief inspector of New Scotland Yard.

"What drug problem?" asked the chief inspector.

The year was 1964. New York City was in the midst of a heroin panic, plagued with the attendant crime wave. And here was the head of Scotland Yard asking, "What drug problem?"

He wasn't kidding. In England drugs and crime were still strangers. Drug addiction was solely a health problem; the cops had nothing to do with it. If you were an addict, you didn't have to rob, mug, or murder to feed your habit—you simply had to show up at a clinic or a doctor's office and you got what you needed. That was the British system.

Now, more than 25 years later, I went to Scotland Yard, asked Paul O'Dwyer's question, and was told that the drug traffic was the No. 1 crime problem in Great Britain.

What happened?

In 1971 the Brits decided to join America's War on Drugs, and they took our prohibition approach, with something called the Misuse of Drugs Act. This law meant arrests, searches and seizures, and draconian penalties for pushers—in short, the works American-style. They didn't abolish the British system—if you can wait long enough, you will get methadone in a public clinic or heroin from a licensed private doctor— but the message went out loud and clear: no more nice guy . . . the English had joined the Western world.

And now the men of Scotland Yard worry that drug-related crime will one day overwhelm their country.

Cause and effect? Or is it simplistic to even ask that question? Can we learn from the British? Have the British learned too much from us? I traveled to London for *Penthouse* to see and hear. And I discovered that when it comes to drugs, the English don't remember where they've been, don't know where they are, and sure as hell don't know where they're going.

That doesn't mean I wasted my time. Read all about it!

The official line in American law-enforcement circles on the British system is that it failed. This conclusion is supposed to end all debate on the legalization of narcotics in the United States. "The English tried it and it didn't work," it's said. And it's said by almost everybody—cops, politicians, and journalists; it's practically a received opinion. Of course, it depends on what one means by "works."

The British system was instituted in 1920 and was never intended to make society drug-free. Addiction was to be treated as an illness. The central idea was to allow addicts to lead useful lives by providing them with maintenance levels of morphine or heroin. There was no suggestion that this would "cure" the drug habits of addicts, nor that it would reduce the number of people taking drugs.

When American experts dismiss the British system, however, they do so on the grounds that it failed to stem addiction, that indeed, more English people became addicted in the 1960's. The experts don't hesitate to connect cause with effect. The Brits gave out drugs, and they got more addicts. Ergo, "The English tried it and it didn't work."

In short, if a system doesn't accomplish what it never set out to accomplish, it is a failure. But prohibition, which has as its sole purpose the suppression of drug traffic, has never succeeded; drugs are a geometrically larger problem in America with every passing year. Yet no one ever points to our drug-prohibition system and says, "The Americans tried it and it didn't work." Nor do you hear this said about the British prohibition of the last 20 years.

Crazy? Of course crazy. But in a world in which we seem to have ruled out any alternative to law enforcement, it is no wonder that we are AWOL from reality.

The question that needs to be asked in America — and in England — is whether providing drugs to addicts significantly cuts the crime rate. Paul O'Dwyer got his answer a quarter of a century ago. I had reason to believe I'd get a fuller answer now that the British have tried both legalization and prohibition. (Legalization really means medicalization: You have to go to doctors. The term is commonly misused, particularly by those who want permanent prohibition. These people scare others into thinking that heroin and crack will be sold to children at supermarkets.)

Anyway, I didn't get a better answer than Paul O'Dwyer. You might say, however, that I wound up with better questions. For the past two decades, Scotland Yard has monitored the British system. In the old days, 1920–1968, British doctors were pretty much on their own; they were trusted to deal with addicts in a responsible manner. The results were fine, with at first a few hundred and later a couple of thousand people using either public clinics or private physicians. Inevitably, given the world drug culture of the sixties, there were abuses—a few doctors were found to have colluded in the rising use of drugs by giving addicts weekly and even monthly supplies rather than day-to-day. A black market, small but discernible, developed, and so Scotland Yard was appointed to check on the physicians and the pharmacists.

For my purposes this was terrific. Since Scotland Yard knew the doctors, the clinics, and the addicts, surely they could answer the jackpot question: Do the people who get the drugs legally commit the usual drug-related crimes of robbery, mugging, mayhem, and murder?

And the answer, from one of the top men who run the show at Scotland Yard, was this: "We don't know." Not only that—I could only get this answer by promising not to use his name. Here is the not-for-attribution quote from the man on the spot at New Scotland Yard:

"We have no way of knowing whether those who receive drugs from the National Health [Service] clinics or 'provide doctors' commit crimes nonetheless. We don't know if they are more or less criminal than those who buy the stuff on the street. The clinics have long waiting lists owing to serious financial cutbacks. We don't know whether that makes a difference in the amount of crime. The clinics don't give injectables; they attempt to wean off addicts through methadone and morphine mixtures and psychological advice. Licensed doctors give heroin and morphine by injection. An addict who can afford to pay can get the 'works' for far less money than on the street, about $20 American to $200 on the street. We don't know if these people commit more or less crimes than the clinic addicts.

"The reason we have no answers is that we have no statistics. The Home Office has never asked for these figures. It stands to reason that those who can get drugs for nothing or for a reasonable fee—we estimate that a quarter of the registered addicts go to private doctors—would not commit crimes to feed their habits. But we can't say it definitively, since we have no numbers."

Did he know why the Home Office (the authority in charge of Scotland Yard) doesn't ask for the statistics?

"I'd have no way of knowing the reason, or if there is a reason," he said.

He hadn't mentioned cocaine. Was cocaine forbidden?

"It's available. Cocaine is listed as an addictive drug in the statute. But hardly any cocaine is given— we have almost no record of cocaine either in the clinics or through the doctors. I suppose that's remarkable. Cocaine is a big thing on the streets, but presumably there's no demand in the system."

How many people in London use the system? He had the answer to this one: "Twenty thousand registered addicts. It's up 56 percent from last year." Obviously, the increase was startling and I guess I showed it. He smiled. "Yes, it's quite on the upswing. We can only imagine how much larger it would be if not for the waiting lists and perhaps the general ignorance of the system itself in the Asian and black communities."

Are the long waiting lists solely the result of the budget cutbacks? Does it cost that much to administer methadone mixtures?

"Well, they say they treat the addicts—they say they give psychological services—and so they have no funds to handle the demand," he said. "But the truth is, they don't treat them—they just give them the stuff. Still, they won't service the masses; they have the waiting lists. I don't know why this is so, but it is the case."

I am not given to British understatement, but after their 70 years of experience with legalized narcotics, would not one have expected more . . . at least in the way of information? If it "stands to reason" that the registered addicts don't commit crimes to feed their habit, wouldn't one think that the British would arm themselves with statistical proof in order to present a model for other nations? Surely the Home Office would offer an explanation.

"We have no figures," said John Webb, spokesman for the Home Office. "It is assumed that the people who steal and commit other crimes for drugs are those who have to pay for it on the streets," he added, echoing the Scotland Yard man.

Tony Breitwell is the deputy chief inspector at Scotland Yard. I cashed my largest London marker to get to this gentleman, who's known as the most savvy cop on the British drug scene. He turned out to be even better than advertised—thoughtful, frank, honest, and outspoken.

In his forties, Breitwell has spent all of his working life as a police officer. Since prohibition of drugs came about in 1971, virtually all of that life has been outside the British system. The first thing I told him was the story about Paul O'Dwyer and the chief inspector of Scotland Yard. The way he looked at me, I could have been talking about another planet.

"It was before my time," he said, finally. And then he said, "I wonder if it was really true, even then. I wonder about saying something like 'What drug problem?' "

"It wasn't Scotland Yard's problem, anyway," I said.

He nodded. "Probably so," he said. "But what makes me skeptical is how things are perceived today. I mean to say, you wouldn't think we have much of a problem now, judging by the attitude and action of our government. Or inaction."

He paused, perhaps waiting for a question. When he didn't get one, he said, "There's no worse problem here now than drugs; it's our principal crime problem. Everyone on the street knows it—every police officer, every drug abuser, every victim, every pusher. We've had a significant increase in violent crimes over the past several years—robberies, muggings, occasional murders. Now crack is in town. It's just beginning, but it's here. And what are we doing?"

We were lunching. He took a moment to work into the pasta. This time I didn't leave the pregnant pause alone.

"I thought you're fighting the War on Drugs, as in the States."

He gave me a wintry smile and said, "We're in a war, but we're not on war footing. We're understaffed, underbudgeted, we're . . . the truth is, we're asleep as a nation. This is like the years before World War II. I'm not exaggerating. The government has its head in the sand. We don't even have statistics to show how serious this problem is, and we don't have them because the Home Office doesn't want them."

I told Breitwell that he sounded just like the Scotland Yard man overlooking the legalized system. He nodded, but he brushed it off. I was to find that everybody involved in prohibition gave no thought to the British system, as if it didn't exist. The English are on two tracks, going in opposite directions.

Without reliable statistics, crime control is a helter-skelter proposition in democratic nations, where money goes to where the problems exist—hopefully. In the big cities of America, drug-related-crime numbers may err, but if so, they err by over-emphasis. In New York, estimates of drug-related crime range from 50 to 70 percent. Such a range is by definition unscientific, but it doesn't really matter, because crime and drugs are virtually a single entry in America. Read the newspapers, watch the television. This is not the case in England, to say the least.

"We don't report drug-related crime in this country," Breitwell explained. "It's not a reportable statistic. For example, when we arrest a known addict in a robbery or burglary, we chalk it up to robbery or burglary. Drugs don't enter into the statistics—there's not even a check-off box on the sheet to indicate drugs. So

the robbery rate goes up, but not the drugs. The public
has no way to know that one thing relates to the other.

"When we deal with direct drug causes, as when
we hit a dealer, we have a hundred-percent clear-up
rate. On its face, this means we never fail, we're impec-
cable, we clear up every case brought to our attention.
But it's a phony statistic. Because we don't record a
drug sale or possession case unless we make the arrest.
Now, in most cases, we simply don't have the man-
power to follow up tips. We can only look into a small
percentage of cases given to us by informants. So what
does it mean to say we clear them all? Next to nothing.
And worse, it gives the impression we are doing things
we aren't doing. So England sleeps."

I asked why he thought the government allowed
this apparent madness. "You said that the Home Office wants it this way."

"They don't want to disturb public confidence."

"But now that they've moved to prohibition, they
must want to do everything within their means to stem
the drug traffic," I said. "Maybe they don't want to
panic the public, and maybe they don't want to empty
the treasury, but what reason could they have to down-
play the issue?"

"Let me give you an example," Breitwell said. "In
1986 we uncovered a major money-laundering operation in London that led straightaway to Miami. The
Drug Enforcement Administration in America was excited by it, and we worked with them on it for more
than two years. At first I was able to put 15 of my men
on the case, and of course I was on it. By the time the
case was broken, we were down to two British officers.
And when the culprits were apprehended, we got no

thanks from the Home Office. The only question they asked was 'What good did it do us?' The case was solved in the States, after all, so why should we care?

"But the Americans appreciated what we did—they knew that without us nothing would have happened. The seizure in America was $100 million, cash money. The D.E.A. has a policy of giving ten percent of all such moneys to helpful foreign governments. In our case they offered us half. Fifty million dollars!

"The 'catch' was that we had to use the money for drug enforcement." He looked at me, waiting for a question again.

"That's a catch?" I asked.

"You laugh. But yes. The Treasury turned down the offer on the grounds that we decide where the money goes. The British government doesn't take orders on allocation of funds from other countries."

"And this went down?" I asked.

"Oh, yes. It made for a question in Parliament, but it went down. A senior Scotland Yard officer said, 'We don't want to be seen as bounty hunters.' So we didn't get the $50 million. That was the final result of Operation Cougar, the title we gave to our finest effort, a pioneering effort in money laundering. And we can't afford to provide pittances to our informants. You can imagine what this did to morale."

"Why did Scotland Yard go along?"

"It is called politics," Tony Breitwell said. "Nobody wants to disturb public confidence."

I wanted to see the street scene, so Breitwell set me up for an afternoon with a veteran detective-sergeant. We did Battersea, in West London. It's the "black" section, and it was not unlike a mini-tour of

Harlem 20 years ago. That is, there was not that much apparent to the eye, but the cops knew where the bodies were. The language was today.

"The blacks are on cocaine, the Asians on heroin," the detective-sergeant said. "They're animals whatever the hell they're on. My wife says I'm a racist, but I'm no racist. I see what I see. These people don't give a goddamn about their families. They're living for the junk—they push, they use, that's what their lives are about. Not all of them, but too many. We've got the same problem you've got in the States, only we don't seem to know it here."

"I'm told they can get cocaine for nothing in the clinics, but they don't seem to know that," I said.

He said, "Who the fuck wants them to know it?"

Prohibition is as prohibition does. Cops on the spot are the same in New York as in London, the same everywhere. Their job is to collar, and they don't want to hear about alternatives. He took me around to spots where the drugs were being dealt, and all he could talk about was the frustration of law enforcement. And who could blame him?

Back in New York a few days later, a friend sent me a clipping from *The Independent*, a London newspaper. It was a letter to the editor, signed Dr. John Marks, consultant psychiatrist, Mersey Regional Health Authority, Liverpool: "For the past seven years (1982–1989), we have revived the old 'British system' of controlled prescribing of heroin, cocaine, and amphetamines at two clinics on the Mersey. The result has been, strange to say, a reduction in acquisitive crime and an improvement in addicts' health, with everyone, except the gangsters, benefiting. . . . By contrast,

America reels under its prohibition. Since we followed American policy, we have reaped the same result and our prohibition has been accompanied by a rise in drug use and the number of drug addicts."

When I related this to a major law-enforcement official in New York, he said, "England tried it and it didn't work."

# IV

## POLS, PRESIDENTS AND CONSPIRACIES

# Bush Is A Dead Bagel

*Inside Straight:* The London bookies make Bill Clinton 4-7, meaning you must lay $7 to win $4. A few months ago, George Bush was 1-2½; you had to put up $250 to win $100. English sportsmen tell me this is unprecedented, easily the biggest swing in the history of the British book on U.S. elections. Nobody can remember the last time the London bookmakers were wrong on our Presidential race. If you think they're wrong now, you can have Mr. Bush at 5-4; you lay $4 to win $5. In case you're wondering how the hell you can get down in sunny old England without TWA, I know a Park Avenue judy who can place all the green you like over there. At no charge, of course, but of course, if you win you owe me one—the marker is mine.

*Jesus Baker:* A California State Senator, in town for the 49ers-Giants game, was saying at Gallagher's that with James Baker in camp, we can expect the Bush campaign to get real dirty. "He's got to go to the gutter to win, and Baker's great in the gutter," said Senator Quentin Kopp. Why should you care what Quentin Kopp says? Because he is the first independent—that is to say, nonparty person—to win a Senate seat in California in this century.

He is also very clear-eyed and sensible, a raconteur, and of course, a maverick's maverick. But this does not mean he has to be right about Mr. Baker, especially when he uncharacteristically mouths the conventional wisdom. Everybody knows James Baker is a gutter fighter, or was in 1988. But that was then, and as they say, this is now.

I think James Baker has his eye on the Nobel Peace Prize. You don't get that baby by running a "we hate niggers" campaign, or one based on "lookee, lookee, here's the bimbo."

Maybe Mr. Baker would go that route if he had a fair notion it could work. But he can check the London book as easily as the next guy. So I see him keeping the President on the high ground.

"But that would sink Bush," Senator Kopp said.

"Indeed."

"So you're saying that the Savior turns out to be the Nemesis."

"He'll give him a good, decent Christian burial," I said.

"That's perfectly cynical," Senator Kopp said.

Then Quentin Kopp ordered a fresh young vodka rocks. He sat pensively until it arrived. And then he announced: "I'm laying the price on Clinton. The election is over."

Any man who takes my word for it, that quickly, no less . . . well, attention must be paid!

Even if I'm wrong on James Baker, it is difficult to see how the President is electable. His only loyal constituency appears to be those *meshugganahs* who carry fetuses around town. They name them now: "This is Charles. Meet Emma." How a man who used to go to the birth control ball in Greenwich managed to corner the market on this crowd is meat for at least a monograph by some ambitious scholar at the Kennedy Institute. Or Sigmund Freud's joint, better.

Just to show you how I get around, or maybe to say that Dr. Freud is just around everybody's corner, I spent a few minutes the other afternoon with an Orthodox Jew named Max Freedman, who is disappointed — crushed! — because Pat Buchanan did not win the Republican nomination. Jews for Buchanan! I asked him if there were many more like him.

"You'd be surprised," Mr. Freedman said.

"Where do you meet, in a telephone booth?"

"It's no joke," he said.

This is Charles. Meet Emma.

# BRAIN-DEAD JOURNALISTS
# (AND A LITTLE ORAL SEX)

The real jokes in the first so-called Presidential debate were the batting practice pitchers posing as serious journalists. No questions about S&L, nothing on Iran-contra, no Iraqgate, no abortion, no Supreme Court, no Middle East, no environment, no draft, no hint that the cracker-barrel billionaire paid millions to his fabulous volunteers—and of course no memory of his quitting in the corner at the first breeze of a missed left hook.

Did these panelists cook it up this way? Did they meet first and decide never to ask an embarrassing question? Did they say, "If it's something the public wants to know, steer clear"?

I wish I had inside information that something like this happened, for it would show a conspiracy, and conspiracies at least imply minds at work. But after what our eyes saw, who would believe that this brain-dead crowd could spell conspiracy, even if we spotted them nine letters?

If these reporters are representative of American journalism, then American journalism is a supine little bed wetter, fully deserving the scorn of a free people.

*The New York Times* blames the format for what didn't get asked at this event. The format was of course lousy. But a format that allows you to throw home-run balls should not prevent you from throwing a couple of strikes. The fact that follow-up questions are difficult to get in hardly justifies the lack of a good first question. I mean, this is first-day-out journalism school stuff—let's forget the apologies.

With a raging Iraqgate scandal threatening to implicate the Bush Justice Department in a loathsome cover-up, we are to be treated to cop-outs about format?

Is the fact that journalism missed the biggest bank heist in history a justification for not saying its name in the presence of a President on whose watch the robbery took place?

On this, the first anniversary of Clarence Thomas-Anita Hill, did the moderator and panel decide that the historic confrontation was old news, or did they just feel that nobody cares about the Supreme Court, anyway?

The next President may have as many as five appointments to the Court, even if he serves only one term, assuming the actuarial tables are anywhere near solid. Since there are no true civil libertarians on the Court today, a Clinton victory promises to get us back on the road cleared by the great Warren Court. If Mr. Clinton learned half of what he was supposed to have learned at Yale Law School, he is a cinch to take the game away from the statists who have been eviscerating the Bill of Rights since Richard Nixon got his hammerlock on our liberties. We know what Mr. Bush will do, but what would we know if we knew only what we learned at the Great Debate?

Saddam Hussein still thumbs his nose at the world, but why bother the President with this detail, when we can put one right in his wheelhouse? Legalizing narcotics? Why, is there a powerful lobby out there in the country pushing for free heroin?

Israel and Bush-Baker were headlines through virtually all of this Administration, with the Israelis taking a bashing unprecedented in American statecraft. But why trouble Mr. Bush about it? Isn't it all too boring, now that he has the Prime Minister he likes in Israel? (Incidentally, here's a scoop: Congress recently passed the full $10 billion loan guarantee to Israel. It awaits the President's signature, which is practically a foregone conclusion. You didn't hear about it as of this writing, because the pro-Israeli Congress didn't want publicity. Where were the reporters? They'll be there when the President does the stroke-of-the-pen thing.)

Nobody cares about abortion, right? So that's why these reporters didn't ask about it. You can understand that—hell, they had only 90 minutes to work with, what do you want?

The environment is for public television.

And Bill Clinton has been asked about the draft; you want great journalists to be *nudges?* Plus the bimbo thing is a scratch now that we know about Jennifer with a J.

But the big surprise was that Sander Vanocur didn't ask Ross Perot why he dropped the Henry for Ross. I *know* why, but you'd have to be old enough to remember Henry Aldrich and "Coming, mother," to dig it.

Hey, look how they turned this half-pint tyrant into Will Rogers, right before our eyes!

You think these ladies and gentlemen of the press are so coarse as to ask him about bugging his employees? Or—God forbid!—did he really say he wasn't about to let his daughter marry some Jew? Or: What the hell are you doing here? Where's the candidate of the Prohibition Party?

H.L. Mencken would have throwed up, baby.

Well, since this whole night was about oral sex, herein a little coitus interruptus for still another scoop: Sydney Biddle Barrows has been giving seminars to the wives of the rich and famous on How to Keep Them From Straying. Ten women to a sitting at a grand apiece. Held mainly in country clubs, I hear. What surprises is that they nailed these moguls without doing that "mouth thing," as Mr. Bush might say, if he were only asked.

Back to the Great Debate, and a remembrance of things past, in case the conventional wisdom convinces you that these magnificent newspapermen and women did the best they could.

It is 1943 in Passaic, N.J., at Roosevelt School No. 10. I am 10 years old, and I am the teacher's pet. So I am the moderator in a debate sponsored by the League of Women Voters. At stake: Who will be the five commissioners of Our Town?

We are instructed by our faculty and by the League of Women Voters to ask only "issue-oriented" questions, which we understood, even at age 10. We also knew that there were no issues in Passaic city elections, just as there were no parties.

As a moderator, I get to ask the first question, which is written out for me by Mrs. Barry, my home room teacher, the one who loves me. It is as follows:

"Gentlemen, what do you propose to do about the Erie Railroad?"

Now, the Erie Railroad has run through Main Avenue forever, and forever every candidate for commissioner has promised to get rid of it in favor of a beautiful park.

Of course, everybody in Passaic understands that the commissioners have as much power to accomplish this as to open a Second Front in Paris.

The next question is from my pal Tony. He asks the Police Commissioner: "How come you took the book away from my father in the Fourth Ward? How do you expect us to live?"

Schnunny from President Street is next at bat: "Mr. Mayor, is it true you got caught with a blonde in your house by your wife?"

As you might imagine, there is nothing but bedlam in the auditorium now. I am immediately replaced as moderator by the political columnist of *The Passaic Herald-News*.

He asks: "Gentlemen, suppose you tell us what separates each of you from the other."

I don't know where Jim Lehrer was that day, but . . .

Anyhow, one last scoop as we pray for the recovery of the American Media come Thursday, Oct. 15.

The London bookies had Bill Clinton 1–3 before the debate. It went to 1–4 minutes later. I got down on the early line, and you didn't. Yo, Sydney Biddle Barrows!

# BUSH'S ANTI-ISRAEL POLICY

Wingy Manone, the one-armed jazz trumpeter, dashed into a haberdashery in Tulsa an eon ago and asked to buy one cuff link. The square behind the counter rebuffed him out of hand. When Wingy got back to New York he told the cats: "Stay out of Tulsa, boys. It's a tourist trap."

I faxed this beauty to Yitzhak Rabin the moment the news arrived that Mr. Bush had invited him to Kennebunkport. Alas. But if Wingy wasn't considered a good enough warning, Dorothy Parker surely provides the metaphor for Israel under the Bush Administration.

At a Halloween party in the Jazz Age, Miss Parker was asked to join a group of merrymakers who were "ducking for apples." Dotty said, "Change one letter in that phrase and you have the story of my life."

It is no exaggeration — it may be understatement — to say, as George Will did in the early days of the Bush Administration: "Never in Israel's 42 years has it faced such an unsympathetic administration."

More recent events make it an understatement. The word is *hostile*. "Unsympathetic" is practically antiseptic when one considers the Bush-Baker record on Israel. Until the other day, I considered it unnecessary to review this record, I was sure that people who support Israel needed no brush-up on what this gang has done to undermine the Jewish state on the ground and in American public opinion. If you care about Israel, these guys get the gate, I thought. It goes without saying, I thought.

Well, as Madison said to Hamilton when Hamilton opposed the Bill of Rights on the grounds that the protections embodied therein "go without saying," Madison put it to him like so: "If it goes without saying, it will go better said."

A line has been running through the Establishment press like a low-grade fever to the effect that Bush-Baker was terrific for Israel, that whatever harshness the Administrative showed was caused by Likud intransigence and was nothing worse than castor oil administered to a recalcitrant child. The end—the "peace process"—justified the means and even exalted it.

I gave this apologia less than one cuff link, it was preaching to the converted. Who but the most fundamentalist peace now-niks would buy that Bush-Baker had Israeli interests at heart, were *pro*-Israel? *Meshugga*.

The other day, the low-grade fever jumped to the intensive care unit. *The New York Times* proclaimed editorially that by the election of Mr. Rabin, the Israeli people had "endorsed" the Bush-Baker peace policy!

Now my blue eyes turned red. Some of my best friends are on the editorial page of *The Times*. But this gives oversimplification a bad name.

There were at least a dozen reasons for the fall of Likud. One surely was the loss of American support for

Israel, though that was hardly as important as the sad state of the Israeli economy. Yes, many Israelis, including many Likudniks, believed that Mr. Shamir had screwed up the peace negotiations and had played into the hands of the Bush Administration, not to mention the critics of Israel in the media. But that is a far cry from concluding that the Israeli people endorsed Bush-Baker.

*The New York Times* is famous for its polls. Let them ask the Israelis whom they would vote for in our election. If Mr. Bush gets more than 10 percent of the vote, I buy the house at Le Cirque. And that includes the Israeli-Arab vote.

It's time to go to the videotape.

Even before they were out of the blocks, Bush-Baker had Israel cornered. The Reagan Administration, in its last five years, had been pro-Israel, at least as much and probably more than any American Government, including L.B.J.'s. In December 1988, however, on the eve of turning the controls over to George Bush, Secretary of State George Schultz announced that the U.S. would begin negotiations with the Palestine Liberation Organization.

This event was inexplicable except as a contract for the incoming Bush Administration. Why suddenly would Mr. Schultz believe a pledge by Yasir Arafat to abandon terrorism, the negotiable instrument for putting the P.L.O. in America's good graces? The thing was a setup, the paper was written in the State Department, and only a fool or a knave would have bought it as truth.

But bought it was and Bush-Baker were off to the races. Or to the turkey hunt. As Mr. Baker put it to

*Time* magazine on the eve of his ascension to State: "The trick is getting them where you want them, on your terms . . . pull the trigger or don't. It doesn't matter once you've got them where you want them. The important thing is knowing that it's in your hands, that you can do whatever you determine is in your interest to do."

The *Time* reporter thought Mr. Baker was referring to the turkey—this was an interview conducted during Jim Baker's annual turkey hunt on the Texas-Mexico border.

"No," said Mr. Baker. "I mean Israel."

Thus began the Bush Administration's terror attacks on Israel, climaxed by the President's "lonely little guy" speech in September 1991 that portrayed the Jewish lobby as an all-powerful force in the Congress dedicated to undoing true American values. All the lobby was trying to do was to hold the Administration to its pledge of guaranteeing a $10 billion loan to Israel to absorb Russian immigrants. The "lonely little guy" managed to unleash an unprecedented anti-Israel, even anti-Semitic, reaction in the country that cowed the Congress and ran off the Jewish Lobby.

What had Israel done to deserve this treatment? Why was the Jewish Lobby depicted by Mr. Bush as the second coming of the Elders of the Protocols of Zion?

During the Gulf war, Israel took 39 missile hits from Iraq. They were told not to fire back by America and like good little boys they did not fire back. The Likud, the terrible intransigents whom we could not do business with, agreed to take 39 missiles on their land.

While the peaceful Palestinians stood on rooftops cheering the missiles.

On the first day of the war, General Schwarzkopf announced that American bombers had destroyed most of the Iraqi missile launchers. It turned out that he had not destroyed even one launcher. The missiles continued to drop in Israel. General Schwarzkopf assured the world and the Israelis that the launchers were finished. More missiles.

At the Yale Club, everybody praised Israel for its restraint. Ditto at *The New York Times.* Israel would get "brownie points" for this once the war was over.

At war's end I met with Prime Minister Shamir.

"Why did you agree to put off the loan guarantees?" I asked him.

"It's not important," he said. "The Americans want to wait until September, they say it will be easier then."

"But now you're popular in America," I said. "How do you know what will happen in September?"

"You're being paranoiac, Zion," said Mr. Shamir. "The Americans will fulfill their word to us, do not worry."

Wingy Manone, where the hell are you now?

□□□
# GUYS I LIKE
□□□

Lately I've taken to saying the three little words: "I like Clinton." Each time I do it, somebody at the bar turns to me with a relieved smile and says, "I do, too." And just like that, we're in a funny little conspiracy— two people not ashamed to say they like the guy they're going to vote for. Imagine it!

Truth to tell, I could not have imagined it six months ago, even three months ago. Hell, the last time I voted without the old clothespin on my shnoz it was for Julius Cinamon and Morris Pashman, 30 years ago in the Passaic City Commission election.

So why, in this Year of the Clothespin, do I hail the kid from Little Rock? Well, I can count the reasons, and I never would have believed that, even two months ago.

Look how he kept truckin'! They threw more stink bombs at this guy than an elephant's clothespin could stanch, and here he stands a week before the election, 2-9 on the London book—forget about the U.S. polls. In June, he was a $2\frac{1}{2}$-1 dog; now you must lay nine on him to win $2. And the only hope George Bush has is the last English election; all he can say is that the Brits swung Tory in the booth, so why not Americans?

How many people, not to mention politicians, would have been left with legs after the Gennifer tapes? Preferring inquiry over rhetorical questions, I discussed this matter telephonically the other day with Mr. James Breslin, always a universal voice on such delicate issues.

"I'd have been out of there before they pressed the button on the Sony," Mr. Breslin said.

What would you have done, baby?

But look what Mr. Bill did. He got his wife to say it wasn't so. On *60 Minutes*, yet. Right then, all the other Democratic hopefuls heard Cousin Joe's song: "You think that you're the only pebble on the sand but there's a little rock in Arkansas."

But he lied, you say? You don't believe he never had anything but platonics with Gennifer? Absurd, you say?

The answer is, 2–9 on the London line.

Of course, after weathering Hurricane Gennifer, the draft-dodging had to be a walk. Alas, Mr. Bush didn't get it, despite his years at the side of the Teflon Man. But then, Bill Clinton makes Ronald Reagan look like snot on velvet, so perhaps we shouldn't be too beastly to poor George.

Now, you may be thinking I've got tongue in cheek here, saying, "I like Clinton." No! A man who can smile through these assaults on his character impresses me. Particularly since I never believed the charges slandered his character.

Do I say he was telling the truth about Gennifer and the draft? My answer, in legal lingo, is, "I demur." Which means, "If so, so what?" At least half the country commits so-called adultery, and more than half the young men of the late 1960's avoided or tried to avoid the Vietnam War.

Bill Clinton understood that the public understood all of this and would not punish him for what their children did then, and what they do every other day. Unless he confessed. Then he'd have been dead in the water.

Instead, he's 2–9 in London. And nobody can remember when the London book has been wrong on an American Presidential race.

I like Mr. Clinton for other reasons, you betcha. And here, I'll number them:

1. The Supreme Court. The next President will likely have several appointments to the Court, perhaps as many as five. All that's at stake here is our glorious Constitution, which has barely withstood the hammering of 12 years from Reagan-Bush. Bill Clinton didn't go to Yale Law for nothing. He'll put people in there who will show a decent respect for our liberties, unlike the statists who have had their way since Richard Nixon. Plus, he will reverse the anti-Bill of Rights regime of the lower Federal courts.

2. Foreign Policy. I don't believe Mr. Clinton will pursue a "forward foreign policy," i.e., interventionism. A lot of people I respect worry about this, but it's to the good, and especially so given our domestic needs. I don't worry about him on Israel, because I see no indication that he is in thrall to the "Wise Men," who somehow always see oil when they look at the Middle East, when they don't see pushy Jews. Generally, he seems without strong ideology, and without Jimmy Carter's "humanism," thank the Lord.

3. The Economy. Who the hell knows about the

economy? What we do know is that Mr. Bush doesn't know how to get us up a couple of inches out of the mess. I cross my fingers that Mr. Clinton will put together a team that will stir it up, and, like they say, "get America moving again."

4. The Environment. Just say Al Gore.

5. The Malaise. Jimmy Carter whacked himself out by saying we were in it, but we're in it now. And there's something about the Comeback Kid that gives real hope here. I mean, just think of how he handled himself in the debates, particularly after the first debate. Swinging and moving, he made J.F.K. look like a stick; you could look it up, you could look at it!

The thing is, if you're for Bill Clinton, get your head up, be happy. I'm no Democrat, nor am I G.O.P., but this guy is the best I've seen, and I'm as old as Red Barber was when Mike Burke fired him from the Yankee broadcasting booth.

Ah, rare Red Barber. He made his mark, of course, with the Brooklyn Dodgers. My old man, bred in B'klyn, was a Dodger fan. Me, the Yanks. The only thing we agreed on in baseball was Red Barber, who got away the other day at 84.

Now here is what my daddy told me about the "shot heard 'round the world," the Bobby Thomson homer in the '51 playoff, Giants-Dodgers.

Everybody watched TV, but my father, a dentist, had to listen to the radio, while doing root canal. He had on, natch, the Dodger station. We all heard Russ Hodges screaming: "And the Giants win the pennant, the Giants win the pennant, the Giants win the pennant!" That was the Giants' station, and we hear it now ad infinitum on the TV reruns.

"Red did it this way," my father told me:

"Thompson swings, it's a long fly ball to left ..."

(The screaming of the fans was all you could hear, said Daddy.)

And then, Red Barber: "There will be no baseball in Brooklyn tomorrow."

Thanks to Jonathan Schwartz, there will be music in New York. There will be Sinatra and Ella and Basie and Rodgers and Hart and Sammy Cahn and Jule Styne and all the old home run hitters. On WQEW, the new call letters for the great WNEW, which was recently sold to a guy who thought the stock market reports were more important than Duke Ellington. Jonathan thought different, and Punch Sulzberger did too.

I like Bill, I like Jonathan, I like Punch.

How about you?

# CHARACTER, TASTE
# AND THE PRESIDENT

ㅁㅁㅁ

The critical moment came on the last weekend of the campaign, when the Gallup poll switched from registered voters to "likely" voters and dropped the race to a dead heat. This caused heart palpitations among many of my friends and relatives. It also meant that money could be stolen from Republicans at decent rates. Assuming, of course, that the Gallup people were crazy.

Therefore, as I always do when easy money beckons and cardiac arrest threatens, I phoned my Cousin Maxie in Passaic.

"You've got 24 hours to flush out the suckers," Maxie said. "By tomorrow the number will change, so act quickly."

"People are scared, Max. My phone doesn't stop since this Gallup poll."

"The election is over, relax."

"You don't think it will be close?"

"The American people are often stupid," Maxie said. "But they are never masochistic."

"Did you make that up?"

"It is my line and I want credit, if that's what you mean."

I'm going to buy him a lollipop and dinner at '21.' This line was so beautiful and reassuring that I ran around town in a veritable frenzy, and now rich Republicans are standing in line with course notes for my palm. They bit for this Gallup poll so hard that I got down at even with a few and never had to lay more than 2–1. In comparison, the London line never went below 1–3 Clinton and the final line was 1–6. And of course, Maxie was right on all points: The Gallup poll moved up within 24 hours and then put it away for Bill Clinton. We are left to wonder about that dead-heat call, but for me, I thank the Gallup organization and invite them back in four years.

Meantime, did you notice that George Bush managed to pull the smallest percentage vote by a sitting President since 1912? The last number I saw was 37.49 percent, which, if it holds after the absentee ballots are counted, would put Mr. Bush a shade under the percentage garnered by the great George McGovern in 1972.

The kaddish for Mr. Bush begins with the economy, of course, and it is almost universally agreed that had the economy been healthy, he would be planning his second term. Sadly, this is the likely truth; history demonstrates that the American people do not stir themselves up to throw out the incumbent when their pockets are full and the future looks bright.

It's too bad, it's terrible when you think about it — after all, doesn't the Bill of Rights count, the quality of an administration, the quality of *life?* But facts are facts, and the fact is, we keep the bastards in when the money is rolling.

On the other hand, we are not masochists. When the money stops, we do not vote for four more years of torture. Unlike the Mother Country. I love it that the Republicans were down to hoping that we were like the Brits. Given an economy that made ours look like the Eisenhower years, the English went Tory anyhow, confounding the pollsters and condemning themselves. Of course, the British system does not guarantee a fixed term; the Parliament can throw out the Government. But still, it's good to know that our nation's founders have been proven right once again — they knew what they were doing when they ran the hell out of sunny old England.

Could Mr. Bush have prevailed despite the stalled economy? Despite Maxie's Law?

Well, suppose the Soviet Union had not collapsed. Would Americans have entrusted the Oval Office to a young man without foreign policy credentials? They did it with a young Jack Kennedy and did it again with an old Ronald Reagan. Kennedy had the far harder task, for sure: Our economy was strong and he was Catholic. Plus, it was a hard sell to make the Eisenhower-Nixon Administration "soft on communism." But Kennedy did it, although he did it with the help of some good friends in Chicago, not to mention Tricky Dick. Ronald Reagan did it with spiraling inflation and the help of a whooshy Jimmy Carter, who couldn't get the hostages back to save his office, and who managed to alienate the Jewish vote despite helping to broker the peace in the Middle East.

The irony that plagues the Republicans today is that they lost the foreign policy issue precisely because the Soviet Union fell. And they have the right to take some credit for the fall. Given the relatively close vote this time, it's possible Mr. Bush would have survived had the Russian Bear survived. And that's pretty terrible to think about, too.

Because the Bush Administration was statist in its every move, statist to the bone. Mr. Bush was hellbent to stack the Supreme Court with people who viewed our glorious Constitution as an impediment to government. Its regulatory agencies continually cut into the rights of the people, from abortion to the environment. Justice William O. Douglas said that the scheme of the Bill of Rights was to keep the Government off the back of the people. Mr. Bush, following Ronald Reagan's lead, turned it around. His scheme was to keep the people off the back of the Government. Statism.

Am I a sore winner? Hell, no. I credit Bill Clinton with running the best campaign in my lifetime. He did everything right even before I knew he did everything right.

Like the other day, when I showed up for lunch at '21' to pick up a bet and discovered that Mr. Clinton was the only Democratic governor in the country to send a thank-you note to Ken Aretsky.

Mr. Aretsky, the brilliantly bespoke chairman of '21,' the man who turned the best saloon in the world back to its former glory, and its food beyond anything we dared to imagine, told me that he had sent invitations to every Democratic governor in the summer of 1990 when the party decided to hold its convention in New York.

"The only guy who answered was Bill Clinton," Mr. Aretsky said.

If I had known that, when Mr. Clinton was off the boards, I'd have put enough down to have a piece of '21.' Not that he showed up, maybe he was too busy to show up, but he answered. And they say he's a hayseed.

"I'm writing him again," Mr. Aretsky said. "I'm hoping he'll come. If he does, he'll be the only sitting President who ever came to '21.'"

Let's judge him by this. And by how he handles the Middle East. The two things are connected, you bet. The only things that matter are character and taste. If you're against Israel, you have no character. And if you disdain '21,' where is taste?

# JACK KENNEDY AND *THE NEW YORK POST*

□□□

Everybody began lunch with martinis in those days and, often as not, it became lunch, but this time the barman was still mixing firsts when a guy ran in and said the President was shot in Dallas. I was a rookie reporter on *The New York Post*, standing there with a couple of veterans, and I had to hurry after them because they were out the door in a flash.

The *Post* then was on West Street, just around the corner from the place where we were about to drink, a good joint called The Firehouse. We rushed into the city room, expecting all hell to be breaking loose, but everything was business as usual—the rewrite bank rapping out copy for the second edition, a few reporters working on overnights.

We went over to the desk and asked Johnny Bott, the city editor, what the latest word was on the President.

"What are you talking about?" Bott said.

"We just heard that Kennedy was shot in Dallas, Johnny."

"Look," Johnny Bott said, "I'm trying to put out a paper, don't bother me."

One of us turned on Bott's radio, and Johnny, who wore a leg brace, jumped up and ran to the wire room like a wide receiver. The clerk of the wire room was a guy named Lou, who held a doctorate in philosophy, which might help explain why he was standing there reading "B" copy about the St. Lawrence Seaway, while the "A" copy was running out the door.

The bells on the "A" wire were ringing like Notre Dame on Christmas Eve, but when asked why this didn't alert him, the Ph.D. said, "The bells are always ringing." He was right, too; every urgent bulletin activated the bells, and to the wire services a cat caught in a tree was as urgent as a cat burglar caught at the Russian embassy.

Paul Sann, the boss, screamed "Stop the press," and this stopped us all in our tracks. Nobody had ever heard these movie lines ring out live. Sann said later that he'd waited all his life to do it, though it's doubtful the dream included nearly getting scooped on the assassination of the President of the United States. And the *Post* would have been scooped by the other afternoon papers, the *Journal-American* and *World-Telegram & Sun*. Sann caught it just in time.

The young doctor of philosophy was barred from the wire room, but he wasn't fired. They sent him upstairs to the library. The editors knew that if they cashiered him, the union would fight it and the publisher, Dolly Schiff, would discover what happened.

After the *Post* discovered that Kennedy was shot, Mrs. Schiff came down to the city room from her perch on the 17th floor and immediately went into the conference room with her brain trust.

The New York press had chartered a plane for Dallas and we all waited around anxiously to see who and how many of us would be sent to cover the biggest story of our time. Then it was announced that Kennedy was dead. Mrs. Schiff and her editors left the conference room with the news that we'd pick it up from the wires, there was no point in sending our own down there now that it was over.

When Jack Ruby killed Lee Harvey Oswald, there were second thoughts. And third, fourth and fifth thoughts. Normand Poirier, one of the top reporters on the paper, was told to pack while they had sixth thoughts. Finally, they shipped Normand to Dallas — and he arrived there in time to catch everybody on the way back to New York.

This wasn't exactly a shot-in-the-arm for morale, but the older reporters took it in stride. It didn't surprise me, the rookie, too much. This was, after all, Dolly's Place, the penny-candy store of the New York newspaper world. About a month after I joined the staff, I beat the whole town to the inside story of the Playboy Club's payoff to politicians and lawyers for a New York liquor license. I nailed it down on a Friday afternoon in an exclusive interview with Hugh Hefner. That meant I would have to write in on overtime.

I was told to come in Monday and write it for page one on Tuesday. I said it would never hold, everybody was after this one. I said I would do it without extra pay, gladly, this was my first big story. I did it Monday, and while I was touching it up the *Journal-American* hit my desk. Johnny Bott said, "There goes your story."

Nora Ephron, who started on the paper in the

spring of 1963, as I did, was on her way home from work one night when shots rang out in Times Square and she saw a man fall. She ran to a street phone and reported the shooting to Mort Schiffer, the night city editor.

"But you're off now," Schiffer said.

"I'm standing right here," Nora said. "A man just got shot and there's a crowd around him. Don't you want me to check it out?"

"You're off now," Schiffer repeated. "Go home, we'll pick it up from the wires."

The victim turned out to be a cop. When that came up on the wires, the *Post* sent half the night staff to find a witness. They found nothing, but so what? Better than overtime, better any time.

Joe Kahn got a call from a guy who said he was about to jump off the George Washington Bridge because his girl had dumped him, but first he wanted Joe to interview him. Joe yelled this over to the city desk. Mort Schiffer looked up at the clock, noticed it was after 5, and said, "Ask him if he can do it tomorrow, on straight time." When Joe related the request, the guy broke up laughing. "Forget it," he said, "I can't leave a world as crazy as this." Joe Kahn checked the wires for days, but no jumpers.

The night Kennedy died I volunteered to call in any stories I came across. I was going to cruise around Broadway and see what people were doing. Johnny Bott said fine, but no overtime, and I called in one that never made the paper and maybe you'll guess why.

The Great White Way was anything but; it was a shroud. All the theaters were dark, so were the restaurants and even the saloons. But in one place the lights blazed: Pokerino, at 47th Street and Broadway. You roll balls into holes in pokerino and there's a guy at the mike calling the winners. The crowd was right out of the old bingo parlors my Aunt Katie used to play from Paterson to Jersey City. I asked the mike guy if anybody here knew the President was dead.

"Ask them," he said.

An old doll was playing hard and I tapped her shoulder.

"Madame," I said, "are you aware that President Kennedy has been assassinated?"

"Sure, and it's a crying shame."

"Well, don't you feel a little funny being here tonight?"

"Who the hell are you to ask?" she said.

"I'm a reporter."

"It's none of your goddamn business, now get out of here!"

A couple of people standing nearby joined in this chorus and I left. Johnny Bott said "Jeezus" when I told him, but he didn't think it was appropriate for the occasion.

All that night I thought about that lady, and the more I did the more I thought she was right not to take my pious gaff.

That Sunday I got to test it out.

The Giants were playing football at Yankee Stadium and CBS had reporters all around the stands hectoring the fans for being at the game. One such hotshot stuck the mike in my face.

"Why are you here, sir!"

"To see my Giants."

"But on this weekend, sir!"

"Why not this weekend?"

"The President! President Kennedy has been assassinated."

"I'm aware of that, my friend, I think I'm aware of that."

"But you apparently see no reason to stay away from a football game."

"Do you think the President would miss a game if I were assassinated?"

The guy went into shock, but Thomas Jefferson would have nodded, and I like to think Jack Kennedy ditto.

□□□

# THE CONSPIRACY THEORY

□□□

Jim Garrison gave the power of paranoia a nice little workout over the last couple of years, but when the cards were finally called yesterday it took the jury a coincidental but significant 50-minute hour to acquit Clay Shaw of conspiracy to murder President Kennedy.

Surely there were moments during the five-week trial when the 12 men tried and true, listening to the procession of prosecution witnesses, must have felt like original spectators at Marat-Sade.

Thus, a "mystery witness" from New York who supposedly overheard Mr. Shaw talking conspiracy at a party turned out to be a man who once finger printed his own daughter before allowing her into the house because his "enemies" had often impersonated his relatives in their efforts to destroy him.

One key witness recalled a "bull session" wherein Mr. Shaw and Lee Harvey Oswald discussed plans for the assassination, but the recall had to be jogged out of him by hypnosis. And like that.

All of which was indeed a far cry from what Mr. Garrison, the erstwhile Jolly Green Giant from Gumboland, was promising on national television, in the pages of Playboy and in numerous background discussions with men of letters and otherwise in his New Orleans digs.

It was Mr. Garrison's contention that he had "solved" the murder of the President. The solution, never fully spelled out but mysteriously hinted at by the Giant, involved a C.I.A. cell made up largely of Cubans, a shooting gallery that featured "triangulation" of shots coming from different parts of Dealey Plaza including a manhole, and even an implication that Lyndon B. Johnson gave the nod to the operation.

Heady stuff indeed for a significant part of a nation that at the start of the Garrison investigation had already come to doubt the conclusions of the Warren Commission which put the sole blame for the assassination on Lee Harvey Oswald.

In fairness to Jim Garrison it must be noted that few who spoke to him during the last two years doubted his sincerity. He apparently believed, to the point of obsession, that the Warren Commission report was a tissue of lies, a sophisticated cover story that had no relationship to what really went into the murder of the President.

Indeed, columnist Max Lerner spoke for many people recently when he noted that it took him weeks to shake off the Garrison spell after a long talk with the District Attorney in New Orleans.

Surrounded as he was by "assassin buffs" such as Mark Lane and Mort Sahl, the Jolly Green Giant was able to portray a conspiracy that for pure theater was virtually unparalleled. Or, in the lyrics of Cousin Joe, the Vieux Carré blues singer, Mr. Garrison had an "Elgin movement would make a rabbit hug a hound."

Yet the fabric he wove, like the suits they used to sell on Delancey Street, couldn't stand up in the sunlight. And this has been a grave disappointment not only to the buffs but perhaps to millions of Americans who believed that Mr. Garrison was on to something very big.

Of course, one does not have to disbelieve the Warren Commission. But the debacle in New Orleans has clearly dealt a significant blow to the conspiracy theory. Concomitantly it is likely that the Clay Shaw case has restored the credibility of the Warren Report in a manner as unforeseen by those who tried to stop the trial as it was unintended by the Jolly Green Giant.

This is not to suggest that the plot theorists will close up shop, for they are missionaries with all that the word implies in terms of resiliency. It is not too much to expect that the world will soon be treated to a revisionist treatise or two on the Clay Shaw trial if not on Mr. Garrison himself. Indeed, one young man was heard to surmise yesterday that it was "conceivable" that Jim Garrison was actually a C.I.A. agent since why else would he have put on such a shoddy case.

Is anybody interested in writing a book called "Catch-22"?

## JFK: The Fantasy

$H$itler was on one wall of this ratty little flat in New Orleans and Chairman Mao looked right at him from another. I must have done a double take, but I wasn't going to say anything. And this clearly bugged mine host, a wiry guy who started jumping around in his jump suit, his eyes darting from wall to wall.

"I suppose you're wondering about the pictures," he said, finally.

"No."

"Let me explain why they're there." He wasn't going to be deterred, this guy. You think I would have said "no" otherwise?

"Now Mr. Hitler," he said, "is up there because he was the greatest speaker in the world. It has nothing to do with politics. I don't share Mr. Hitler's politics. But I was a speech minor in school and I admire him as an orator."

He went off in a bit of a trance with that and after about a minute or two I said, "And how about the fellow across the way?"

"Chairman Mao," he said. "You see, I believe that we must build a Chinese Wall around the United States to protect us from communist infiltration. I'm

185

with General MacArthur on that, 100 percent. In order
never to forget it, I keep Chairman Mao's portrait on
my wall."

The only thing I forget is the guy's name. But all
you need to know is that he was Jim Garrison's key
witness in the fabulous J.F.K. assassination trial the
District Attorney staged in New Orleans in 1969. If you
were around then, you might remember that he was
the one who recalled a "bull session" wherein the defendant, Clay Shaw, discussed plans for the assassination with Lee Harvey Oswald, a recollection, alas, that
had to be jogged out of him by one of Mr. Garrison's
hypnotists.

You will not meet this guy in Oliver Stone's *JFK*,
don't worry about it, nor will you get to see the "mystery witness" Mr. Garrison imported from New York
with great fanfare. This one testified that he overheard
Clay Shaw talking conspiracy at a party. On cross-
examination, however, he allowed as how he once fin-
gerprinted his own daughter before allowing her into
his house, because his "enemies" had often impersonated his relatives in their efforts to destroy him.

After five weeks of this kind of proof, the jury took
a coincidental but perhaps significant 50-minute hour
to acquit Clay Shaw of conspiracy to murder President
Kennedy. And there, most observers thought, went Jim
Garrison, the Jolly Green Giant of Gumboland.

I didn't think so, and for once I can prove it.
Writing in *The New York Times* on March 2, 1969, the
day after the verdict, I said: "It is not too much to
expect that the world will soon be treated to a revisionist treatise or two on the Clay Shaw trial, if not on Mr.
Garrison himself."

It took 22 years, so sue me. But bragging has nothing to do with it, anyway. I never believed the Warren Commission. Jim Garrison gave it some credibility, but it was clear the commission's conclusions couldn't last. Who could buy Arlen Specter's pristine bullet theory? (At Loews Columbus Circle the other night, the crowd applauded when Kevin Costner, as Mr. Garrison, blasted Mr. Specter, then a young lawyer with the Warren Commission, as one of the greatest liars of all time. Anita Hill lives!)

I should say how I happened to be in the Hitler-Mao apartment and when. It was in the fall of 1968 and I wasn't on assignment from *The New York Times*. I was there for *Ramparts*. Warren Hinckle, the eye-patched, bad-boy editor of the then hottest magazine in the country, was about to do a cover story extolling Mr. Garrison. But he was a little worried about it, so he asked me to check him out.

Going in, I was hip that Mr. Garrison was a spellbinder. Everybody who had been down to talk with him—and just about every major columnist and reporter *had*—came away mesmerized. Max Lerner said that it took him weeks to shake off the spell.

But even knowing that, I practically had to be hosed down after three hours with the amazing District Attorney of New Orleans parish. Wow! As my man Cousin Joe, the great Vieux Carré blues singer would say, he had an "Elgin movement would make a rabbit hug a hound."

My assignment was to shake it off, and so I insisted on interviewing his major witness. It took a couple of days, and a call from Warren Hinckle, to get Mr. Garrison to give me the fellow with the Hitler picture on his wall.

Once I saw that one it took a minute to tell Mr. Hinckle to drop it, case closed. And he dropped it; no *Ramparts* cover story.

Well, the years go by and by-and-by we get *JFK* in living color. And witness Kevin Costner instructing the jury in the Clay Shaw case that John F. Kennedy was killed by a conspiracy that included the C.I.A., the F.B.I., the National Security Council and the "military-industrial complex." With a nod from Lyndon B. Johnson.

Why?

Because John Kennedy was going to end the Vietnam war.

This is exactly against the evidence.

The critics of the movie have made this point with impressive documentation. Lyndon Johnson did not—as the film has it—change Kennedy's policy, he implemented it. By the time of the assassination, J.F.K. had run 16,500 American troops into Vietnam. Three weeks before Dallas, Kennedy had South Vietnam's President Diem removed in a coup. Kennedy left him to his killers because Diem was working on a peace deal with the communist regime in North Vietnam.

And give us a break that the money men had him whacked because they needed the war to fill their pockets. Those guys, said to be the "permanent government," are either in jail today or in bankruptcy court. The Soviet Union is dead, but Karl Marx lives in Oliver Stone.

Why were we in Vietnam?

I got a story for you.

In 1969, James Reston, lately become Executive Editor of *The New York Times*, wanted to meet some of us young guys on the city staff. Steve Roberts, who had clerked for Scotty in Washington after Harvard, hosted a small dinner party. Richard Reeves and his wife, Steve's wife Cokie, me and wife. I think that was it.

Over coffee and brandy, Scotty said: "Didn't I ever tell you why we got into Vietnam?"

We were all ears, you betcha.

Mr. Reston said that while he was covering the summit conference in Vienna in the spring of 1961, somebody slipped into his hotel suite. "I was fixing myself a drink, and this guy with a hat came in the other door, I thought it was a burglar. The guy dropped into the couch and in that unmistakable voice said: 'Scotty, give me a drink.'"

"It was the President," Mr. Reston said. "And the first thing he told me was, 'Khrushchev raped me today.'"

Kennedy explained: "He has no respect for me because of the Bay of Pigs. That means he has no respect for our country. What do you think I should do, Scotty?"

Mr. Reston gulped.

The President said: "I have to show him we're not gutless. The only way to do it is to send troops into Vietnam. We have advisers there now, it's the only place where we are directly facing the communist threat. I've got to do it, Scotty, it's the only way."

James Reston tells this story in *Deadline*, the memoir he just published. A few details are changed, but you could look it up, Oliver Stone, you could look it up.

◱◱◱

# THE HISS CASE

◱◱◱

In 1969, while launching the muckraker magazine *Scanlan's Monthly*, I received an excited call from writer William A. Reuben, who then — as now — was the world's foremost encyclopedia on the Alger Hiss case.

Reuben told me that a young Smith College professor named Allen Weinstein was about to deliver a paper to the annual meeting of the American Historical Association in Washington. The word, Reuben said, was that Weinstein would cast serious doubt on Hiss's conviction for perjury in connection with charges that he had passed secret State Department documents to the self-confessed communist spy Whittaker Chambers.

This interested Bill Reuben, who then — as now — was the world's foremost advocate of Alger Hiss's innocence. The idea that a scholar in his early thirties — in knee pants when Hiss was tried in 1949 — was asking questions about the case before a prestigious body of historians looked like a big story to Reuben. Would I send him down to cover it, with a view toward perhaps publishing Weinstein's paper in the magazine?

I said okay and Reuben was off to the races; so, in

191

effect, was Allen Weinstein, though hardly in the way any of us figured at the time—Weinstein included.

His paper was generally favorable to Hiss, whose guilt he found "unproven beyond a reasonable doubt." On the other hand, "it would be folly to call him innocent at this point," he said.

This was hardly hot stuff for a new magazine on the make; nor, despite Weinstein's obvious grasp of the complexities of the case, did it break new ground—as he conceded.

So we passed, but in 1971 a slightly revised version of the piece was published in the *American Scholar*. It made no ripples.

Now, Allen Weinstein has created big waves. His book *Perjury: The Hiss-Chambers Case* charges that Hiss was indeed guilty, not only of perjury; he was, says Weinstein, a spy for the Soviet Union.

The response from critics left, center, and right—from Irving Howe to Garry Wills to Bill Buckley—has been overwhelmingly favorable. As Alfred Kazin put it: "After this book it is impossible to imagine anything new in this case except an admission by Alger Hiss that he has been lying for 30 years."

Weinstein's book is seen as different from others of a similar ilk because its author is advertising himself as a man of left-liberal origins who set out to prove Hiss innocent and changed his mind after reviewing thousands of pages of documents obtained via the Freedom of Information Act aided by the American Civil Liberties Union.

Moreover, his "switch" was aided and abetted by his study of Hiss's own files, turned over to him voluntarily by Hiss himself.

So the book quickly took on the aura of received

opinion, and there it might have stayed except for Victor Navasky and that old nemesis of any who would bury Hiss, William A. Reuben.

Navasky, the new editor of the *Nation*, conducted a "mini-investigation" into Weinstein's scholarship. He wrote to seven key sources cited by the author, asking if they had been correctly quoted in the book. Six answered that Weinstein had distorted part or all of their quotes.

Then, working with Reuben, whom he calls the "computer," Navasky contradicted Weinstein's research regarding ten people prominently discussed in the book.

The most telling immediate result: an addendum to Christopher Lehmann-Haupt's favorable review in *The New York Times*. Because the *Nation* raised "serious questions" about Weinstein's objectivity, the book—rather than settling the 30-year "ideological battle"—appears to be "just another incident in the war," Lehmann-Haupt concluded.

Last week, I witnessed a new skirmish in the war, conducted in the radio studios of WMCA under the auspices of Barry Farber. The contestants were Reuben, Weinstein, and Navasky.

I could not detail what went on during the show in any way that would make sense to any but the hardest of the hard-core aficionados of the Hiss-Chambers case.

The show served, however, to remind me of Weinstein's 1969 paper—where, presumably, it all began. Returning home, I checked my old *Scanlan's* files, with little hope of finding the manuscript; but there, miraculously, it was. And a good thing, too, because I was in for a surprise.

In the piece, Weinstein went into great detail concerning what he correctly referred to as the "central mystery" of the case. Briefly, the mystery revolves around the date on which Whittaker Chambers quit the Communist Party.

This is critical, because the evidence that cooked Hiss was certain papers produced by Chambers and submitted by the prosecution as the "immutable witnesses" against Hiss. These papers were copies of State Department documents alleged to have been typed on an old Woodstock typewriter once owned by Hiss.

These documents dated from January 1 to April 1, 1938. The trouble, so far as Chambers's credibility is concerned, is that he had on many occasions over many years said — *sworn* — that he left the party prior to April 1938.

Indeed, Chambers — who had been making allegations against Hiss (and many others) since 1939 — had until the eleventh hour insisted that he quit the party in 1937. He later changed the date to early 1938, and finally, at trial, he made it April 15, 1938.

"The dates involved are important," as Weinstein wrote in his 1969 paper, "because if Chambers had actually broken with the party at some point prior to April 1938, he could not possibly have received the final batch of typed documents from Hiss, and the supposedly immutable witnesses might suddenly begin to scream 'fake.' "

Having noted this, Weinstein proceeded to marshal "abundant evidence" that Chambers broke with the party in either February or March of 1938.

"Thus," Weinstein concluded, "*two* sets of 'immutable witnesses' appear in the Hiss case. The first involves Chambers' break with Communism sometime before mid-March 1938; the second, a collection of State Department documents allegedly stolen by Hiss but dating through April 1, 1938. The discrepancy between these two facts, until satisfactorily resolved, remains the episode's central mystery."

Well. Given this analysis—and it is certainly a cogent, persuasive one—you would have to believe that Weinstein solved it, and to Hiss's detriment, otherwise how could he now conclude that Hiss was guilty?

Amazingly, however, Weinstein does not deal with this "central mystery" in his book—much less solve it. Gone from the book are the discrepancies so well noted in the paper. The only thing Weinstein does with the mystery—if he can be said to do anything with it—is to fudge over one aspect in an appendix note.

So, then, the *new* "central mystery": How did Professor Weinstein manage to "change his mind" without resolving the old central mystery?

I can't answer it, but Barry Farber said something to Weinstein at the close of the show that perhaps will help. "Did you really," Farber asked, "set out to write still another book proclaiming Alger Hiss innocent?"

If Weinstein did, somewhere along the line that question may have occurred to him.

# ALGER HISS, ESQ.

**M**r. Nixon always understood that the gods were up to something with him. He was not one of those lucky ones with the perfect swing; not for him to spend the night with Johnnie Walker and expect to hit three homers in the afternoon. But if you cannot be the Babe you could be Gehrig, you could persevere, learn the tricks of the trade, accept the daily tests, take nothing for granted. The gods would punish but they would also reward and always there was the promise of redemption.

Even in what the world naturally viewed as his final disgrace, Nixon never lost hope. We are told now that he began stirring at Christmastime, working the Wats line like an underwriter looking for the final big ones to put over the new issue. He made two hundred calls around the country and whatever he said the message had to be clear to him: I'm back, I'm alive, don't count me out. Shortly the rumors began. Nixon would like to do something to help his country in foreign policy, his "strong suit." Ambassador to Peking, maybe? No? Well, perhaps too early, but how about the Republican party, could he be of service? Still too early, eh? Maybe next year, yes next year. And now the word that he is planning a long visit to the sights of his foreign glories, a detente hop through the old hated communist conspiracy, with stops at Russia, Poland, China, Bulgaria. Ironic? So what? Everything Richard Nixon ever touched turned to irony and so why not, this once, let it work for him.

Loathe and despise him as you will, it remains next to impossible not to whistle at such gumption; who among us would raise his head after what Nixon has lived through. Yet for all that extraordinary track record in psychic survival, it is hard to believe he can "hang tough" against the resurrection of Alger Hiss.

Alger Hiss readmitted to the Massachusetts Bar, while Richard Nixon fights against disbarment in New York, his legions negotiating—begging is the more likely word—with the Brahmins of the legal establishment to permit him to resign! There is no vocabulary for this, irony melts in the hand, analogies pale and ultimately fail; finally, you must say it's as if Alger Hiss were readmitted to the bar and Richard Nixon was given the gate.

For those of us who were children when it happened, it is not pleasant to contemplate that there are now children who never heard of the Hiss case. I will not attempt to summarize it here; suffice it that Hiss, a former top aide in FDR's State Department, was convicted in 1950 of lying when he denied passing secrets to Whittaker Chambers, on behalf of the Communist Party and the Soviet Union.

The conviction of Hiss, at his second trial (the first ended in a jury deadlock) helped considerably to pave the way for the Cold War; as A.J. Liebling put it, "Hiss's forced conviction shaped American political life for the next five years, 1950–1955, and powerfully influenced it for five more, 1955–1960." Had Liebling lived to see Nixon elected in 1968, he undoubtedly would have amended the statement to bring it up to at least the second Nixon presidency.

The Hiss Case was the lynchpin of Nixon's career, as Nixon himself has often stated. It was Nixon, then a young congressman from California, who "made" the case, shepherding the generally-discredited Chambers through every difficulty. The name Richard M. Nixon, Liebling wrote, "shines out like four fireflies in a bottle," in the Hiss affair.

"The only public impression that Nixon had made in three modest years in the House," Liebling said in The New Yorker, "was through his association with the House Un-American Activities Committee's investigation of Chambers charges against Alger Hiss."

If Chambers had lost, i.e. if Hiss had been acquitted, Nixon would have been "wiped out," according to Liebling, and according to everyone else, including Nixon, who said virtually the same thing, from a different angle, in his book, "Six Crises."

Today, after twenty-five frustrating, terrible years, Alger Hiss is within inches of having his honor fully restored. Once law clerk to Oliver Wendell Holmes, Hiss at 71 can again practice his profession. And this news came within a week of the sensational revelation that the "Pumpkin Papers" contained nothing but garbage. The bulk of these papers, reduced to microfilm and dramatically scooped out one night from a pumpkin on Chambers's farm in Maryland, was kept secret from Hiss and his lawyers all of these years. Yet they were a media event which lined up public opinion harshly, to say the least, against Hiss. Now, due to the Freedom of Information Act, we were all able to inspect this so-called evidence of Hiss's treachery, which Nixon had hailed as the proof of the nation's greatest internal conspiracy.

And there was no there there, as the poet said about Hollywood. The Pumpkin Papers contained such vital material as the kind of life preservers the Navy used on boats in 1937.

It goes without saying that no one can buy back a man's honor. Alger Hiss has won it back by sticking to his guns, by never becoming embittered, and by surviving long enough to catch a little good luck. I hope somebody sues me in Boston so I can hire him.

# PROFESSOR COREY BURIES THE ROSENBERG JUDGE

There's nothing funny about death, I don't have to tell you, but the audience sometimes has its moments. My Aunt Malvina was 75 when her mother passed, and I can hear her screams today: "I'm an orphan! I'm an orphan! Where is God?"

So Professor Irwin Corey, the world's foremost authority, shows up at the private visitation in Frank E. Campbell's for Irving R. Kaufman, the "Rosenberg judge," the night before the funeral. Professor Corey is not there to honor the deceased or comfort the family. He double-talks for a living, but when it comes to Judge Kaufman his single thought is to disrupt the reverie. He has awaited this occasion for 40 years, or ever since Irving Kaufman put Ethel and Julius in the chair.

"You have no idea what terrible things I want to do on that coffin," he tells me later, and then he tells me what, but I will not tell you.

What happens, however, is that the moment Professor Corey sets foot in the room, he is surrounded by Irving R. Kaufman's relatives.

A less courageous man might have felt somewhat menaced by this circling of relatives, for only a couple of days earlier, on what turned out to be the last night of Kaufman's life, Professor Corey threw a fund-raiser at his Sniffen Court digs for the National Committee to Reopen the Rosenberg Case. At this party, Ethel Rosenberg Appel, Julius's sister, called on the gods to preserve Judge Kaufman so that he would live to feel all the pain and suffering she wished on him.

But Irving Kaufman's relatives probably did not know about this bash, nor of the many times Professor Corey rose up in public meetings to explain that the person who just suggested that the Rosenbergs might have been guilty of turning the A-bomb over to Russia was nothing but a "fascist pig rat bastard" who surely did not deserve to live.

Anyway, it does not seem the judge's relatives knew; all they wanted to say, each of them, was how terrific Professor Corey was, how much they admired his work, how wonderful it was that he was here to pay his respects to Irving Kaufman.

"How do you know Irving?" an elderly woman asked, while pressing the professor's arm. "Did Milton Berle introduce you?"

When Kaufman was a young lawyer, Milton Berle was his client. In 1948, Mr. Berle was asked to entertain at a March of Dimes benefit at the Waldorf-Astoria. Irving Kaufman would hear nothing of it. The March of Dimes meant polio and thus was associated in the public mind with the late President Franklin D. Roosevelt. Sensing that in postwar America, F.D.R.'s image had turned pink, Irving Kaufman was not going to allow Milton Berle, his client, to expose himself to such controversy.

But chances are, the elderly woman knew nothing of this history. She likely thought that inasmuch as

Milton Berle and Professor Irwin Corey were both Friars, it figured that Milton Berle put Professor Corey together with Judge Irving Kaufman.

In the event, however, Professor Corey said, "No."

"Then how do you know Irving?" a nephew persisted.

"How does anybody know anybody?" Professor Corey answered. "Nobody can really know anybody in this world, you know that."

Of course, what Professor Corey knew was that by this show of affection, Kaufman's kinfolk had ruined his plan to wake up this wake. As the late law clerk Israel Schawarzberg was wont to say: "They pulled his teeth and now he could only gum them."

Yes, he said many things about the deceased that one does not hear at such affairs, especially when surrounded by the deceased's relatives. But now he had to say these things with a smile, for clearly these relatives loved Professor Irwin Corey even more than they loved the deceased.

"I tell them I never agree with a thing this guy did or a thing this guy said," Professor Corey says proudly. And then he says: "But they beam. Whatever I say about this guy in the coffin, they beam, it's as if I'm praising the bum!"

It is a phenomenon well documented by the Jungians. It is known colloquially as the Awe Factor. The most famous recent example took place in the Knesset when Anwar Sadat made his historic journey to Jerusalem, A.D. 1977.

Sadat demanded that Israel relinquish "every inch" of Arab land occupied since the Six Day War. The applause shook the walls of the Knesset.

The Awe Factor. The Israelis weren't listening to his words, they were enthralled by his presence.

Even Professor Corey can't double-talk his way out of a Jungian archetype.

"Yeah, but I know where they buried him," he says.

# V

## BLACKS, JEWS, GREEKS AND SINATRA

# THE JEFFRIES JIVE

W here I grew up, we lived under Willy's Law, which held that if a guy called you Jew bastard you were to kiss first, talk later. It meant you had to kiss the bum hard enough to land him on his back, where you could put your foot on his throat and say, "Explain!"

This was Passaic in the 1940's, and Willy Rudnitsky was a guy with a heart big as his left hook and he gave us an out. If the sonofabitch was bigger and older than you, Willy would take care of him. But if after checking out the guy he decided you could have kissed him, Willy would take care of *you.*

There has never been a more effective way of combating anti-Semitism, and no finer, the Anti-Defamation League notwithstanding. Try to dialogue with a Jew-baiter or any other form of racist and you lose, by definition. Willy is gone, alas, and the Jew-baiters have changed color and it's done now from college classrooms and lecture podiums, but however fancy it gets it's the same and Willy's Law lives. Kiss now, talk later, even if you can't find the bastards on the streets.

In that spirit, I take up the celebrated case of the Hon. Leonard Jeffries Jr., Doctor of African-American Studies at the City College of New York, who I assure you would not have gotten to the door in good old Passaic.

Dr. Jeffries, of course, is the well-established black bigot who made headlines the other day by his assertion that a conspiracy of Russian Jews and mafiosi had "planned and plotted and programmed out of Hollywood" the "destruction of black people." He even named names, "Greenberg and Weisberg and Trigliani," by which he must have meant Sam Goldwyn, Bugsy Siegel and Lucky Luciano, and would probably have said so had they taught him linear history in college.

Obviously, the main thing the Jews and the Mob had in mind in the halcyon days of Hollywood was putting their money and power behind the ruination of the blacks, everybody knows that. What else was there in La-La Land?

For this commonplace remark, made last month at the Empire State Black Arts and Cultural Festival in Albany, Dr. Jeffries received a standing ovation from his peers. That it took a couple of weeks to make its way into the white establishment press only proves that the ofay media continues to dis black intellectuals. The Festival was not only public live, it was broadcast in full on Albany cable.

When finally *The New York Post* got hold of the transcript, the fan was hit, and poor Jeffries is undoubtedly wondering what he did wrong. After all, as he put it, he got his info from the "head Jew" at City College, whose name he seems to be protecting out of reasons of privacy if not scholarship, uh-huh.

It turns out that Dr. Jeffries has been making witness on this theme for many years, albeit with variations to suit the setting. "Change Hollywood to the

Sociology Department and I've heard this line 50 times," a City College professor told me. "We're so used to Jeffries, we roll our eyes when he opens his mouth. To us he's a schmuck, but maybe we should have taken him more seriously."

They should have taken him to the wall, the first time he outed with his fabulous theory that the skin pigment melanin gives blacks intellectual and physical advantages over whites. If a white professor said the exact opposite, he'd be gone before you could pronounce tenure and we'd hear nothing about academic freedom and the First Amendment. I mean, if this stuff is O.K. with the powers that be at City College, they ought to name the library after Jimmy the Greek, who got whacked off the screen for saying blacks were better athletes because they were bred to have big thighs.

Another wonderful fact uncovered by Dr. Jeffries and his legions is that the Jews ran the slave trade out of Africa, and I think I have a story that might fit here. At the Friars Club some 50 years ago, a little Italian guy got mad at George Jessel for something and threw him against the pool table. "You goddam Christ-killer!" the guy screamed. Jessel said, "Who, me? I was with Gus Edwards at the time."

The initial reaction of the educational authorities to the Jeffries Jive left me wondering whether they were auditioning for the second coming of Tom Wolfe's "Mau-Mauing the Flak-Catchers." Those who said anything seemed unable to get by that dear old standby "deplore," a word that has no more impact on the psyche of Leonard Jeffries than a plain fact has on his mind-set.

Once *The New York Times* got on the scoreboard with the story, you could feel some backbone growing, and sure enough after a week of heat the big dogs at the overseeing City University of New York blasted Dr. Jeffries and promised a probe that could lead to disciplinary action against him.

Even as the trustees were meeting, I was on the phone with Thomas Sobol, Commissioner of Education. Dr. Sobol had been under the gun for weeks before the Jeffries story broke, owing to an advisory committee report advocating an Afro-centric teaching of history that in a word was cookaloo. His office informed me that he wouldn't be interviewed about the Jeffries affair, relying instead on a statement he had issued, the key phrase of which was "most unfortunate." That made "deplore" look strong as rent, but I told his director of communications that all I wanted to know was if the commissioner was a Jew.

Nobody in the press had popped that question, perhaps because everybody assumed he was Jewish, just look at his name. But why would it matter, you ask? Because half the Jews I know were calling me or buttonholing me with the same line: "The worst is this guy Sobol. Did you ever see such a self-hating Jew?"

I had read, however, that his father was Polish, and here's where my Passaic nose began to itch. Passaic was loaded with Poles when I was a kid, and somehow I thought Sobol with two "o's" didn't have to mean Jewish. That excited me, because if I was right I might have the first documented case of a self-hating Pole!

In no time flat, Pat Keegan, the director of communications, called and said as follows: "Mr. Sobol says he is not self-hating, that in fact he feels pretty good about himself. He is not Jewish. He is an Episcopalian. His brother is an Episcopal minister. He is married to a Jewish woman."

I said, "You sure he didn't convert?"

Two minutes later, Thomas Sobol rang me up. He has a New England accent, which didn't have to mean anything since he comes from around Boston. But right away I knew he was not and never had been a Jew.

"My father was a Polish immigrant whose name was Sobolewski," he said. "He shortened it around the time I was born. I never knew any name but Sobol. My father was a Catholic, my mother a Protestant, and I was raised in the Episcopal church."

"O.K.," I said. "But 'most unfortunate'? Is that appropriate for a guy who is apparently teaching this garbage to kids in a state university?"

"I didn't want to fan the flames of hatred," he said.

If I had bade him bye-bye right then, I'd have had my self-hating Pole, I'd have made history.

But I pushed and he went on the record with this: "What Jeffries did was bad in every way, it was hateful, it was totally false, terrible."

I asked what he was going to do about it.

"It's not directly in my purview, but we do have an overseeing capacity. Right now the Chancellor is meeting with the trustees and I'm waiting for their report. In any event, I assure you we will not let this pass."

Did he really tell a black group that he was sorry he was born a white male?

"An absolute lie."

Was he for this Afro-centric curriculum?

"Absolutely not, and I put it in writing."

Was he conning me? A lot of my friends will think so, and all my enemies. Time will tell. Of course, if he was juking me, Willy's Law applies immediately.

# Booze and the Jews

R ev. Al:

The Jew media will do everything to suppress the truth, but there is no question that the Jews are responsible for the derailment of the IRT train that killed and maimed African-Americans in Union Square. The key is Dewar's White Label, the Scotch that the fuzz says deranged the tragic African-American motorman, Robert Ray, causing the crackup of the train.

White Label is imported into the apartheid United States by Schenley Industries, a Jew-controlled operation from the get-go. Schenley was founded by Lewis Rosenstiel, friend of the notorious Jew Roy Cohn and husband of a woman who ran off with Walter Annenberg, whose father was Moses Annenberg, collaborator with Arnold Rothstein in the origination of the international crime cartel that had as its generals Meyer Lansky, Bugsy Siegel, Dutch Schultz, Dutch Goldberg, Longy Zwillman, Doc Stacher and Nig Rosen, whose name alone shows how the Jews dissed African-Americans long before Louis Farrakhan was born.

In recent times, Schenley came under the control of Meshulem Riklis, the Jew-swipe who backed Men-

achem Begin and bankrolled Ariel Sharon, who destroyed Palestinians in Jew-held Lebanon in 1982.

Meshulam Riklis married a woman half his age
and turned her into a singer and then got Frank Sinatra
to put her in as warm-up for his act, and Frank Sinatra
of course was sponsored by Lucky Luciano, who gave
Italian cover to the Jew crime cartel. Frank Sinatra is
married to the ex-wife of the late Zeppo Marx, of the
notorious Marx Brothers, who did movies with the
vicious Tom Bojangles, who used to dance on the top
of the dugout at Yankee Stadium to amuse the apartheid Yankees led by Joe DiMaggio, who married Mar-
ilyn Monroe, who left him for the Jew Commie Arthur
Miller, who never found time to write a play about
African-Americans though he did expose the Jew mu-
nitions maker who sold out airmen for gelt, though he
never mentioned that the Air Force was apartheid.

Of course, we must be prepared for Whitey to say
it wasn't Dewar's White Label, but this is playing into
our hands should they try it. Seagram's sells plenty of
Scotch in its never-ending Jew conspiracy to destroy
African-Americans, and I remind you, Al, who owns
Seagram's. None other than Edgar Bronfman Sr., who
is only the head of the World Jewish Congress!

The Bronfman family comes out of Canada, a
country whose very existence as an independent opera-
tive was a ruse to protect the Jew rum business during
Prohibition. Canada is nothing but an armpit of Amer-
ika, populated entirely by Ice People, and so was a
perfect cover to pour booze into the unsuspecting
gullets of our Sun People.

Prohibition, of course, came in under the auspices
of the Jew Woodrow Wilson, maiden name Itzy Wolin-

sky, the man who underwrote the notorious Balfour Declaration, which created the so-called State of Israel, now financed by Meshulam Riklis, Edgar Bronfman and their guinea cohorts Gambino, Colombo and Lucchese.

The beauty part for the Bronfmans was that being in Canada they were not subject to American law. They made the booze destined to destroy Black America, but they were not accountable. What they did was to deliver it a few miles in the water from Malone, N.Y., where the Jew Dutch Schultz was tried and bought off his jury, and then it was up to Longy Zwillman, Meyer Lansky and the others to bring it to Harlem.

The Jew E.L. Doctorow said nothing about this in his paean to Dutch Schultz, "Billy Bathgate," published by Random House, which is owned by the Newhouse empire, whose political power was midwifed by Roy Cohn. This Doctorow is under the control of Victor Navasky, who edits *The Nation*, which pretends to support the Palestinians but is owned by Arthur Carter, who owns *The Observer*, which promotes the right-wing Jew Hilton Kramer, who wrote for *The New York Times*, run by the notorious Jew family Sulzberger.

I may be getting you a little dizzy but you know me, Al. I'm a freak for history, so, Al, bear with me, the Jews don't make it easy to explain. But this is the way we have to do it, scholarship, it's not enough to do like Sonny Carson, though I don't want to name names.

Our scholarship leaves no doubt that the money that fueled Harry Cohn in Hollywood came out of Prohibition hootch. Dutch Goldberg, who later fi-

nanced the Irgun, which wiped out Dir Yassin, sent
Bugsy Siegel to Hollywood to create Stepin Fetchit.

But they made a mistake. Stepin Fetchit never
took a drink! He was Tomming from the heart of a Jew!
Jews don't drink, everybody knew that then and everybody knows that now. What to do?

The Jews knew just what to do. They made role
models out of the goyim. Do you know, friend Al, how
many black people became drunks because Nick and
Nora were on Beefeaters?

Now the Jews tell us that our real enemies are the
goyim. They say, we're victims like you, they say the
goyim want to set us against each other, Jew against
Negro, Jew against black, Jew against African-
American.

Some victims, the Jews. Are we supposed to believe that the Episcopal Bishop of New York runs
Crown Heights? Or Cardinal O'Connor?

And then they say we've got the Mayor of New
York, David Dinkins. They say that to us, while they
say to each other they elected him.

Yeah, they elected him. They voted for him
to keep us down, they figured he'd make sure the
shvartzes wouldn't run up Park Avenue, are you kidding? You know me, Al, and you know I'm right.

David Dinkins, give me a break. The Jew Shuberts
have got him booked for the road show of "Driving
Miss Daisy."

On the other hand, friend Al, if we keep the heat
on him we can make half the Jews think he's us. I
mean, you did it in Crown Heights, you got him to tell
the cops to duck. For three days the cops stood around
while Sonny Carson's kids rapped the shit out of the

Jew bastards and out of the coppers. Duck, that was the order from the Tom police commissioner.

Eventually he copped out, Dave the Dude, the Jews got to him. But I got to say for him, he wouldn't dis you. The Jew media wanted him to whack you out, but no soap, so to say, and I know the Holocaust weepers will make the most of that line.

We got to beware, however, that they will try to connect this IRT accident to the Jew bastard who ran the light in Crown Heights. After all, they are liable to say, our guy had no alcohol in the test while your guy, Robert Ray, was plus-positive. Our guy, they'll say, didn't leave the scene, while your guy hauled ass.

But that's why, Al, we have to be ready with the scholarship. With Schenley Industries and Seagram's.

And if they pull the crap that there was a crack vial on that train, we have the answer too, again they'll be playing into our hands.

Do you know who first imported cocaine into the apartheid U.S. of A.?

Dopey Benny Fein, Monk Eastman, Lepke Buchalter, Gurrah Shapiro, Pretty Amberg and Jewcetera.

They all worked for Arnold Rothstein, who got his front money from Irving Berlin, who wrote "White Christmas."

You know me, Al.

Your pal,
Dr. J

# POGROM IN BROOKLYN

I magine that a Mercedes driven by a Jew ran a light on 57th and Park, got sideswiped, jumped the curb and killed a black child.

Imagine that a crowd of blacks surrounded the Mercedes, beat up the Jewish driver and, when he was rescued by the police, made a run on Temple Emanu-El and started pelting it with rocks and screaming "Heil Hitler!"

Imagine that hours later a posse of blacks grabbed the first Jew they saw in front of Le Cirque and stabbed him to death.

Imagine that for three straight nights thereafter, black mobs laid siege to Temple Emanu-El, burned Israeli flags, cried "Kristallnacht!" and continued to pelt the synagogue and the police guarding it with rocks.

Imagine that the Police Commissioner ordered the cops to duck, under policy guidelines informally set by the Mayor.

Imagine that throughout these three days and nights, blacks roamed Jewish neighborhoods, smashing windows and heads at their pleasure.

Imagine all that, and then imagine the reactions of the great Jewish defense organizations — the Anti-Defamation League, the American Jewish Committee, the American Jewish Congress.

They'd take down the thunder from the skies, that's what they'd do—if it happened here. Every top leader from everywhere in the country would fly into town, there'd be round-the-clock sessions with the Mayor, there'd be hell to pay if anybody caught a cop ducking—if it happened here. And if it happened here it would be over quick, there'd be no three nights of siege and roving mobs.

But of course it didn't happen at Temple Emanu-El on Fifth Avenue, it happened at the Lubavitcher shul on Eastern Parkway in a forsaken part of Brooklyn called Crown Heights.

And it didn't happen to Jews who are at home at the Four Seasons or bespoke by Morty Sills. It happened to Jews whose idea of high fashion is 16th-century Vilna, who wouldn't drink a glass of water in your average kosher restaurant in Manhattan, who wear beards and yarmulkes under their black hats. They are mostly poor Jews, too, Jews who don't believe in abortion or birth control, Jews who believe in God and their Rebbe and—God forbid!—the Messiah.

For these Jews, the great leaders of the great Jewish organizations did nothing and said next to nothing. For the first time in history a Jew was lynched on the streets of New York, and the great Jewish leaders didn't even come to his funeral.

For nearly two weeks from the day the riot broke out and Yankel Rosenbaum was lynched, the only thing we heard from the great Jewish defense organizations were some faxed-out verities calling for racial harmony.

"We perceived it as a local issue."

Thus said Abraham Foxman, executive director of the Anti-Defamation League, and I'll tell you the context and place of the remark after I note that Mr. Foxman was the man who broke the Jewish organizational silence with an extraordinary press conference in which he admitted that the A.D.L. had made a mistake by its virtual inaction in the face of this most serious outbreak of anti-Semitism.

I use the word "extraordinary" advisedly and I'm sure understatedly. It may have been the first time in recorded history that a Jewish organization admitted fallibility.

Here's the place and context, as promised.

On Sunday, Sept. 1, I went to Crown Heights to meet with Rabbi Yehuda Krinsky, the longtime spokesman for the Lubavitchers and an old friend. There were several people sitting with Rabbi Krinsky when I arrived, including Abe Foxman, but he waved me into his office. Mr. Foxman was doing the talking and the first thing I heard him say was as follows:

"You could have called me, Rabbi. You know my number, you could have called me. It works both ways."

He went on that way for a minute or two. Rabbi Krinsky listened intently, being a sophisticated man and a fine diplomat.

Finally, he said: "I don't see that it works both ways, Abe. There was a pogrom going on outside these windows and in this neighborhood. Jews were being stabbed and robbed, they were throwing stones through Jewish windows, people were afraid to walk the streets, afraid to go home. The police were told to do nothing, to duck. Eighty or ninety policemen were injured, some of them seriously. It was a pogrom."

Yehuda Krinsky paused, he looked Abe Foxman in the eyes and he said: "I'm sorry, but under those conditions it didn't occur to me to pick up the phone and call the Anti-Defamation League."

Abe Foxman said: "We perceived it as a local issue."

I piped up at that one.

"You wouldn't have perceived it as a local issue if it happened at Temple Emanu-El," I said.

Everybody nodded. Rabbi Krinsky smiled, and not thinly this time. But Abe Foxman didn't nod and surely he didn't smile. He said, "That's a good line, Sidney."

"It's only a good line because it's true," I said. Everybody nodded. They were not Hasidim sitting around the table, strictly secular Jews, I want to get that straight lest you think I was talking to a cheering squad of black hats.

And I make this point lest anyone think that the Jewish leadership necessarily represents the Jews of New York or anywhere in this country for that matter.

This is not personal to Abe Foxman, who may be the best of all of them. But nobody elected any of them to speak for Jewry, and that includes Abe Foxman.

Wherever I went during this pogrom I was beset by Jews who were outraged at what was happening in Crown Heights. And not just Jews. In the saloons of New York, where few Jews congregate, alas, Irish and Italian and WASP's were at one in their heat at what was happening out there in Brooklyn. None of them asked what the Jewish leaders were doing, they wanted to know what David Dinkins wasn't doing.

They were right, of course. The Mayor could have been a hero had he gone on television and attacked the hustlers and charlatans who cynically turned a tragic accident into a pogrom. Had he done that, had he enforced the law immediately, had he said that he was not elected to be a black mayor but the mayor of all the people of New York, that the hit men and self-promoters were delivering black children to hell, David Dinkins would have been hailed as a great man and you can be sure his picture would have run on the covers of *Time* and *Newsweek* and *U.S. News & World Report.* Not to mention on network news.

Instead—well, we know too well what he did instead.

What the Jewish leadership didn't do, we do not know well enough.

When they say nothing they send a message, particularly to news organizations. Journalists automatically call the leadership for comment, and when there is no comment who can expect the papers and television to get exercised?

It produces echoes of the Holocaust, when the Jewish organizations joined in the conspiracy of silence dictated by the Allied powers with Franklin Roosevelt at the watch. The Jewish leadership in those dread days delivered the Jewish vote to F.D.R., who smoked Camels while the Jews of Europe went up in smoke.

We hear the pledge Never Again and we hear it again and again.

And then the "wrong Jews" get it in the neck and we hear nothing.

Except the terrible echoes of German Jews in the 30's. They looked at the Jews of Poland, Lithuania,

Latvia, and thought, hey, look at them, they're not us, they're an embarrassment to us, what do we have in common with them?

The lime kilns answered them. The Jews, in Ben Hecht's deadly phrase, had the "unity of a target."

It can't happen here, and I don't say that ironically.

But something happened in Crown Heights that ought to make us all wonder why the hell we need these great Jewish organizations.

# UNLIKELY ALLIES:
# JEWS AND JEWS

❏❏❏

D avid Dinkins may not realize it, but Fail Safe has arrived when the Jewish establishment's anxiety over him exceeds its embarrassment over the Hasidim.

The signs that such a messianic phenomenon is at hand were strewn all over the Mayor's gorgeous mosaic the other day, in the wake of his rush to judgment that the beating of a black man on the premises of the Lubavitcher yeshiva was "repugnant." Mr. Dinkins blamed the Hasidim, with whom he has been feuding for more than a year, and his Police Commissioner labeled the incident a "bias crime," even before an arrest was made.

Had both of them cooled it for an hour or so, or as long as it takes to pull a rap sheet out of the computer, second thoughts might have saved the Mayor from the ensuing onslaught by mainstream Jews and, surely, from the reluctant shaking of heads by his pals, the Jewish leaders.

Because the rap sheet on the black man, Ralph Nimmons, is an arm-and-a-half long: Robbery 1, Robbery 2, Burglary, Criminal Trespass, Petty Larceny—six convictions all told since 1986, with sentences running from 15 days to two-to-six years.

This record, plus the fact that Mr. Nimmons left nine burglary tools on the premises, lends credence to the Hasidim who say that he was caught trying to burglarize a yeshiva. To say the least.

If this does not necessarily justify the beating, if the people who jumped on Mr. Nimmons went too far, it in no way justifies the ballistic reaction of Mayor Dinkins and Police Commissioner Raymond Kelly. To put it in some kind of perspective, Yankel Rosenbaum was in his grave before the police called his murder a bias crime.

Why did David Dinkins rush to judgment? Pete Hamill wrote in *The New York Post*—and incidentally the *Post* deserves credit, hands down, for the best reporting and editorializing on the incident—that Mr. Dinkins was reacting as a black man, just as he, Mr. Hamill, would have reacted as an Irishman to reports of British torture in Belfast, or Jews to anti-Semitism. Mr. Hamill does not excuse Mr. Dinkins; he tries to understand him as a human being. And this may be all there was to it, for of course David Dinkins is anything but an anti-Semite.

But I think there was more to it. I think Mr. Dinkins jumped the gun because he was anxious to defray criticism of his reaction to the obscene verdict in the Yankel Rosenbaum case. Against all of his previous judgments on racially induced verdicts, Mr. Dinkins defended the jury that cleared the alleged killer of Yankel Rosenbaum. When he heard that a black man was beaten up by his prime critics, the Hasidim, he saw it as a terrific opportunity to separate the Lubavitchers from the Jews of New York.

And this, I believe, has been his strategy ever since

he came under attack for his handling of the Crown Heights riots in the summer of 1991.

The Jewish establishment has been his silent ally in that endeavor from the beginning. When the accidental death of a black child triggered four days of rioting by blacks against the Hasidim, when the Lubavitcher shul was under siege, Jewish leaders took to the sidelines. Yankel Rosenbaum was murdered on the first night. David Dinkins called it a lynching. But the rioting continued and the cops for three nights did nothing. And the Jewish leaders said nothing. The Lubavitchers correctly called it a pogrom, while certain Jewish politicians were busy explaining that a pogrom had to be officially arranged, as by the Czar.

Definitions aside, the cops ducked for three nights, as blacks threw rocks and Molotov cocktails. When Mr. Dinkins showed up and was showered the same way, the cops suddenly found their power, and the riot was over in a trice.

Everywhere in New York, Jews were outraged—and not just Jews. I am perhaps the last Jewish drunk since Toots Shor, which means that I hang out at bars with Gentiles. And they were plenty mad. But the Jewish leadership was calm. After all, who the hell are these people with black hats and curls? I wrote then, in this space, that if it had happened at Temple Emanu-El, every Jewish leader in the country would have been on the spot in hours, and the Mayor of New York would have declared martial law before he would allow marauders to have their way with the fine Jews. If Yankel Rosenbaum had been killed outside of Le Cirque, forget about it, baby.

Mr. Dinkins insists, with great heat, that he never

instructed the police to duck, to back off in any way during the riots, and he demands that those who say so prove it. It's an irrelevant defense, else what's bureaucracy for? And meaningless in light of the Mayor's acceptance of responsibility for the "tactical errors" of the cops. It is this kind of talk that is turning Mr. Dinkins into the Ray Handley of New York politics. All bureaucrats, like all executioners, are alike. They know what is expected of them.

The trial of Lemrick Nelson for the murder of Yankel Rosenbaum took place 14 months after Rosenbaum's death. The cops caught the suspect on the spot with a bloody knife, the suspect confessed and the dying Rosenbaum identified him.

A few nights after the jury acquitted the defendant, I ran into Dick Gallagher at J.P. Clare's saloon. Mr. Gallagher is a retired homicide detective, one of the best in the history of the Finest. "What do you think?" I said.

"When you get a suspect with a bloody knife in his pocket," he replied, "and then he confesses, and then the victim identifies him as the killer, and the butler was off that night—it's a wet dream."

So why?

"Check the jury," Dick Gallagher said.

And the jury was composed of six blacks, four Hispanics and two whites. No Jews.

When David Dinkins defended the jury, like a regular Cardozo, he was praised by *The New York Times* and embraced by the Jewish establishment, including the Board of New York Rabbis.

But the Jews knew better, the real Jews, and so did the Gentiles, many of whom told me that if this could happen to the Jews, what would happen if a black mob killed an Irishman, or an Italian?

But David Dinkins felt secure in the embrace of the Jewish leaders. And so he thought he had it all when he heard that a bunch of Hasidim beat up a "homeless" black man on the steps of the home of the Lubevitcher Rebbe.

And then the Jewish leaders, for the first time, heard the voices of the Jewish people. And stopped trying to be Rabbi Stephen Wise in relation to Franklin Roosevelt.

One more like this and who knows? Balfour Brickner and Ruth Messinger and Rita Hauser might be out there with Dov Hikind. Never Again!

□□□

# BIGOTRY ON THE SIDE

□□□

Here is a scene that could not have happened a couple of years ago—even a year ago.

I am at a dinner party in the Hamptons. There are 10 people at the table and I don't know half of them. One of these, a woman on my left, asks me what I am up to. I tell her I'm writing a book on Israel.

"What kind of book on Israel?" This is not the woman on my left asking. It is a man across from me, whom I have just met.

"It is called *Israel Without Guilt*," I say. "If that gives you some idea." I smile sweetly. It is the last smile of the night for me.

What followed, from two-thirds of the table, was an attack on the Jewish state that is best described in this funny lingo: A left hook to the head, a right cross to the chin, a left and right to the midsection, an uppercut to the jaw, three straight rabbit punches and a head butt.

Why do I say this couldn't have happened even a year ago? Israel-bashing as sport has been going for at least 10 years, right?

But this time I was the only Jew in the room.

Some of my best friends are Gentiles. Until now, I

had to depend on them to tell me what the Gentile world was saying about Israel or about the Jews. With my name, forget about my map, no Gentile would utter a seriously hostile word about Jews or Israel to me. Even in *vino*, only very occasionally.

There was one night at the Yale Club when an Old Blue on his sixth Rob Roy upped to me and said: "How do you feel about the Jews robbing this town blind?" This was at the height of the Donald Manes-Stanley Friedman scandal.

"Now why would you ask me a question like that?" I said.

"And I damn well want an answer from you, too," he said.

The others at the bar, including the barmen, either froze or turned away. You could hear a pin drop.

"Do you really want to know?" I said. "Or are you just defending your black belt as the leading anti-Semite in the Yale Club?"

The old gent's face turned lobster, he glared hard—but he ran the hell out of there. Except for a couple of Jews who got a little nervous about my effrontery, the rest of the crowd seemed as pleased with my riposte as they were dismayed by his conduct. People shook my hand, clapped my back.

Now for all I know, this guy said what the rest of them were thinking. But I don't go around thinking people are anti-Semites. They've got to say or do something to prove it before I even consider them for this calling.

My iron law holds that only a Jew can decide if a person is an anti-Semite. You can't join such a company of gentlemen and scholars just because you talk or write a good game. We're supposed to let any little *shtunk* in there with Voltaire and F.D.R.? Unless you have impact, kiddo, the best you get is a kick in the teeth.

Of course, if you make the cut you're in forever. No heartfelt denials will help and don't bring around an affidavit from the B'nai B'rith, either. I'll get to where you might think I'm going, don't worry about it, but first I want to take you back to the dinner table.

I have heard worse attacks on Israel, believe me. But always from other Jews. And until fairly recently, it was almost invariably in an all-Jewish setting. The unwritten rule was that you didn't fight it out in front of Gentiles. This is known as a *shonda* for the *goyim*.

I never subscribed to this school of thought, but that's the way it played out. This changed with the *intifada*, but even so, the Gentiles were generally quite careful in conversation, their criticism of Israel practically gentle. Picking a fight was out of the question. What they said to each other—who knew? With us in the room, nobody got rough, except us against each other.

So when it got going hard at that dinner table, I was at first amused. Then I was bemused. By the end of the evening I got it through my thick skull that something big had happened.

It was now strictly kosher for Gentiles to blast Israel right in my face!

With the exception of the hostess, whom I was meeting for the first time, the word Jew never surfaced, everything was Israelis: Why are they so brutal to the Palestinians, why won't they give them their land back, why should we give them loan guarantees while they occupy Arab territory, etc.

Finally the hostess outed with this one: "Jews say

they're the Chosen People. Why don't they act like it, instead of acting like Nazis!"

This did not go over well with the table, I hasten to say. And I add that throughout the dinner, a couple of the guests argued *for* Israel, though without anything like the heat that was coming the other way.

I said to my hostess: "Could I have heard wrong, or did you say something a little anti-Semitic?"

"Anti-Semitic?" she said. "How could you accuse me of that! How dare you!"

"Well, this Chosen People stuff, and Nazis . . ."

To break the tension, I guess, a male guest said: "Just because one criticizes Israel does not make one an anti-Semite."

You hear that all the time, and of course it's true. But a school of journalists and television commentators have upped the ante: Just because you're anti-Israel, they say, doesn't mean you're anti-Semitic.

My first answer to this is as follows: Just because you're anti-Israel doesn't mean you're *not* anti-Semitic.

But my real answer is that if you're anti-Israel, I don't ask whether you're an anti-Semite. Because if you are truly anti-Israel you are an enemy of the Jewish people. Therefore I don't need to calibrate the spit.

I don't think, in other words, that it is legitimate to be anti-Israel, any more than it's legitimate to be an anti-Semite.

You knew I was going to get to George Bush and James Baker, didn't you?

No American Administration has done more to legitimatize anti-Israelism than this one, it's not even a close call. The reason is simple: They have conducted, from the outset, an anti-Israeli policy. There are apologists everywhere bending over backwards to say it isn't so, but all they can get is a sacroiliac condition.

In the Gulf war, Bush-Baker forced Israel to take 39 missile hits without firing back. The excuse was that only thus would the Arab coalition hold. But every Arab state, except Jordan, which backed Saddam, announced that Israel would have every right to respond to a missile attack.

Israel took the shots and zoomed up in the public opinion polls. They'd get big brownie points for this. And then and there, because Israel was popular, Mr. Baker asked them to delay the request for loan guarantees to absorb the Soviet immigration. Mr. Bush announced that the guarantees would not be linked to the settlement policy in the West Bank.

The rest is history, culminating in Mr. Baker's alleged "Fuck the Jews." Whether he said it or not, what else has he been doing? And now the leaks come: Israel has been selling our technology to the Chinese, they say.

All of this has emboldened the anti-Israeli hitters in the media. As usual, the press listens to the loudest voices.

Only I didn't think it would reach a dinner table in Sag Harbor. Not with me there and all those Gentiles.

Am I getting old, or just dumb?

# CALL IT SLEEP

In 1970, Sheik Mohammed Ali Jaabari, the Mayor of Hebron, had a few of us American journalists to his home for tea. Those were the days when every news-paperman who went to the Holy Land hunted for moderate Arab leaders who might help broker a peace between Israel and Jordan and thus end the three-year occupation of the West Bank and Gaza. Mayor Jaabari seemed the quintessential moderate: He not only was close to King Hussein but despised the Palestine Liberation Organization.

I have reconstructed the interview from memory and from talking with a newsman who was present.

Sheik Jaabari was asked the jackpot question first: What do the Arabs require for peace?

"It is quite simple," he said. "The Jews will have to restore to the Arabs all the land taken from them in the wars."

I said, "Did you say 'wars'? Not the 1967 war, but 'wars'?"

"All the wars — everything since the U.N. partition plan of 1947."

"That would mean Jaffa, for example."

"Yes," Sheik Jaabari said. "There were 70,000

Arabs in Jaffa in 1947; there will be 70,000 Arabs in Jaffa now."

"And half the Negev, and part of Haifa, all of Jerusalem, Beersheba."

"The whole of the Negev," he said. "And, for sure, Jerusalem, and much of Haifa, and Beersheba. Wherever the Arabs were then, the Arabs will be now."

I said, "Mr. Mayor, if the Israelis were to accept this arrangement, would you then recognize them and make peace with them?"

He thought for a moment and said, "I assure you that if the Jews do this, the Arab leaders will be very favorable to them."

"But no guarantees in advance," I said.

"The Arab leaders will have to meet, of course. But I know them. I know how they think. I tell you they would be very favorable to the Jews."

"First, the Israelis must give back the land and then the Arab leaders meet, is that it?"

"Yes, though it might be simultaneously — that is a detail."

"Anyway, the Israelis must make the offer unconditionally."

"For peace, absolutely."

I said: "Mr. Mayor, I have great respect for you. So please do not take what I must say as a sign of disrespect."

"Say anything you like. You are my guest."

"My question is, What would your terms be if you *won* the war?"

So you wake up 17 years later, you read the papers and watch TV, and what do you know! If only the Jews hadn't been so brutish to the fathers, the sons wouldn't be throwing stones and Molotov cocktails at Israeli soldiers. What the Jews could have had from the moderate fathers they won't get from the sons. The sons are now filled with fury, rage, frustration and cannot be controlled by their dads, whose compromising ways have proved fruitless. The Israelis missed the boat, media barons say, and when they say it, the consensus lines up around the corner.

The Middle East memory bank is empty again. It goes belly up every time Israel gets rough with its enemies. When this happens, the world is born yesterday, or tomorrow.

In 1981, Israel took out the Iraqi nuclear reactor. The Israelis were carpet-bombed by the world media, which had never heard of the hanging gardens of Baghdad: What right did the Israelis have to do this to good old peace-loving Iraq? And how dare they invade Lebanon? That Syria and the P.L.O. had established a police state-within-a-state in Lebanon was forgotten: The Israeli hordes were overrunning a beautiful nation.

Yet none of the foregoing is as galling as this latest book of genesis, which has it that Israeli intransigence is responsible for the West Bank riots. Because now we are told to forget everything: that the Six-Day War was provoked by Egypt; that Hussein fired the first shot in Jerusalem after Prime Minister Levi Eshkol begged him to stay out, in a taped phone conversation—the only war in history where history can prove that history never had to happen; that from that moment on, the Arabs knew only one word, no.

And not just from *that* moment. Had the Arabs accepted the partition of 1947, Israel would be a fragment of what it is today, and very likely a memory. Had the Arabs been satisfied with the pre-June 1967 boundaries—the boundaries they now say they want—there would have been no Six-Day War.

The one time an Arab leader said yes—Anwar el-Sadat—Israel gave him everything he wanted.

The critics of Israel pretend to know nothing of this. They mount a moral attack on the Jewish state, many of them equating Israel with South Africa—as if the blacks had gone to war against the whites, had vowed to destroy them. It is a profoundly vicious analogy, without a scintilla of factual basis, but like all big lies it grows and grows.

What if these moral cynics had their way? Suppose there was a Palestinian state in Gaza and the West Bank? Does anybody believe the Arabs would be free? There's not a free Arab state in the world: "Self-determination" is nothing more than a code word for the right to be ruled by a dictator of your own race. But then the moral critics of Israel could sleep, close the book on the Middle East—as they have on Vietnam, Cambodia and black Africa. If Israel becomes history—well, that's the price of sleep.

# SABRA, SHATILA & IRAQ

ꓱꓱꓱ

Let us remember Sabra and Shatila as we witness the carnage in Iraq. There are similarities to be observed, differences to be digested and lessons to be learned.

On the night of Sept. 16, 1982, Lebanese Christian Phalangists entered the neighborhoods of Sabra and Shatila—commonly called "refugee camps"—in the suburbs of Beirut. This was shortly after the Israeli military had driven 10,000 PLO fighters out of Lebanon. It was only two days after terrorists had assassinated the newly elected president of Lebanon, Phalangist leader Bashir Gemayel.

In the aftermath of the assassination, Israeli intelligence reported that 2,000 PLO terrorists had managed to stay in the country, many of them now back in Sabra and Shatila. Concerned that they represented a threat to Beirut, the Israelis asked the Phalangists— who had done next to nothing to free their land of the PLO—to flush the residue out.

The result was a massacre that included as victims women and children, both Palestinian and Shiite. Death estimates ranged in the hundreds. The Christians, long the targets of terrorism, had more than settled some scores. It was nothing less than a blood-bath. But the blame fell not on the Phalangists. World condemnation landed directly on Israel.

In America, Sabra and Shatila became household words. Thousands of newspaper articles, TV reports and photographs made plain the atrocity. ABC produced an hour-long documentary. *Time* and *Newsweek* ran cover stories, and U.S. journalists won Pulitzers for their coverage. The verdict was virtually unanimous: Israel had behaved much like its age-old enemies. Power had corrupted its Jewish soul.

In Israel, the *mea culpas* sounded a Yom Kippur wail. A judicial commission, headed by the president of the Supreme Court, held the high command "indirectly responsible" for the massacre. The powers-that-be should have foreseen what the Phalangists would do, should have stopped the slaughter the moment they should have known it was happening.

Israeli Defense Minister Ariel Sharon was forced to resign, as was his military intelligence chief. A few months later, Prime Minister Begin left office and went into seclusion, saying, "I cannot bear it anymore." The blot on the reputation of Israel was practically indelible. Even today, those who may have forgotten the names Sabra and Shatila know that Israel did something terrible, something that all but extinguished the biblical ideal of a "light unto the nations."

What has all this to do with America's conduct in Iraq, with today's news?

The similarity should be obvious: Arabs killing Arabs while armies that could stop the carnage stand by and do nothing.

What are the differences?

The worst that could be said about Israel was that it looked the other way while its enemies were being massacred by its friends. America, looking directly at the killing field, allows its enemies to destroy its friends — or if not its friends, those it encouraged to rise up and oust its enemy, the worse-than-Hitler Saddam Hussein.

In numbers, the difference is in kind. We are talking about tens of thousands killed by Saddam Hussein — not the couple of hundred in Sabra and Shatila — while we look on and discuss interests of state, as we leak assurances we'll get Saddam later, once he has put down his civil war.

Imagine if Israel had done anything close to what we do now. If the Israelis had said that to encourage stability in Lebanon they would deal with the Palestinians and Shiites on the basis of benign neglect. If Ariel Sharon announced that he could not interfere with the internal affairs of Lebanon. If, thus, the massacres had continued.

I know I will be accused by some of leaving out the real differences: Israel asked the Phalangists to go into the camps while we, of course, made no such request of Saddam. It is a distinction, to be sure, but of negative moral benefit to America. The Israelis should have known; when they knew, they did stop the carnage. We also should have known that if we didn't destroy Saddam's war machine he would commit genocide. And we don't stop it.

What are the lessons of Sabra, Shatila and Iraq? Is it just that we are hypocrites, that we demand from Israel what we do not demand from ourselves, much less the Arab world? It is all of that, but it is more.

Let us be humble, a little bit, as we approach the New World Order. Let us not continue to instruct Israel about morality. Let us understand that the Middle East is not necessarily subject to our usual analysis, our way of thinking, our notions of justice. Let us know, in this Passover-Easter season, that we have learned war, but not peace.

ㅁㅁㅁ

# MACEDONIA & SINATRA

ㅁㅁㅁ

Athens—The first time I came to this cradle of civilization, I was run into a quarantine room at the airport and vaccinated by a guy who had the face of a gulag guard and the touch of a middle linebacker. In those days, you had to travel with a pass from the World Health Organization, and mine lacked the proper notary stamp, so said the keepers of the cradle, forget about it that my arm sported a vaccination mark plain as the Parthenon.

That was in the summer of 1970, when the Colonels' junta was in full flower. I didn't really need the vaccination to know that these thugs had worked up a pretty good police state on Plato's stomping grounds, the air itself told the story. Then I lunched in an outdoor cafe and the faces in the crowd provided all the confirmation I needed. The *retsina* didn't go down too well. Nor did the feta cheese, when I saw the fear all around me and realized that this junta was being nurtured with great pleasure by our very own Nixon-Agnew gang. The Sixth Fleet was right there to protect these Colonels, and I thought, what's a nice Jewish boy doing in a place like this. I grabbed the next plane to Geneva.

The junta fell in 1974, at around the time Mr. Nixon got his last ride on Air Force One, but the stench of that afternoon stayed awake in my nostrils. I was right next door in little old Israel a couple of dozen times in the next couple of decades and still never dropped over to sunny old Athens. When asked, I would answer, "As soon as they recognize Israel." It seemed a little like waiting for the Second Coming, the country had turned into a haven for P.L.O. hit men.

Well, good things happen to patient Jews, not to mention patient Greeks. Two years ago, a genuine Greek hero, Constantine Mitsotakis was sworn in as Prime Minister. Mr. Mitsotakis had as a youth fought the Nazi occupation, managing to survive two arrests and death sentences. When the Colonels grabbed the country in 1967, they immediately put him under house arrest. He got away and lived in exile, returning after the junta went down. He served in various high governmental posts until finally, at age 70, he became Prime Minister. With a wave of the hand, he recognized Israel.

And now here I was the other night shaking his hand in the garden of his private home.

I told him about my quick getaway the last time I saw Athens and how different the city felt today.

"How long have you been here?" he asked.

"Five hours," I said.

He smiled.

"Well, it didn't take but a minute," I said. "You can smell democracy quick as you can smell dictatorship."

He nodded, and I thought to myself that this was pretty good chutzpah, me telling him about that.

"Congratulations on recognizing Israel," I said. "Why did you do it?"

"Why not?" he said.

I have questioned more politicians across the years than I like to admit to my children. Never have I heard so fine an answer.

Mr. Mitsotakis deserves the same kind of answer from President Bush on Macedonia, but all he's been getting is let's-have-lunch, and that's putting the best spin on it.

Macedonia? What?

It is the birthplace of Aristotle and Alexander the Great. This should make it Greek, wouldn't you say? But Marshall Tito hijacked the name, and part of the region, after the Second World War. Now, with the breakup of Yugoslavia, the 2 million people living there, most of them Slavs, want to keep the name — they want to call their newly independent state the Republic of Macedonia.

The Greeks, of course, have their own province of Macedonia. They refuse to recognize this new Slavic state if it insists on the continued expropriated use of the name.

The Greeks are united on this issue, a rare thing, and for good reason. This isn't a matter of vanity. Tito's move triggered a civil war in Greece that claimed the lives of 100,000 people. Unless Mr. Mitsotakis wins on this, his two-vote majority in Parliament is gone. Since he is easily the best friend America has had in Greece for years — he delivered in Iraq, he made a naval base agreement with us, he is tough on terrorism — one would think we'd be with him on Macedonia, hands down. If he goes down, the Socialists are back, and the Socialists hate America.

Naturally, I asked the Prime Minister why he thought we weren't coming across for him on this issue. He said he didn't know and I don't think he was being entirely diplomatic. Because I don't think the Bush Administration knows. What I really think is that they dismiss Greece, they look at numbers, these guys of ours, and they say, what can they do to us. Not even, what have they done for us lately.

What would H. Ross Perot do?

On the flight over to Athens, I had Cole Porter on my mind. "Let's fly away/Let's find a land that's warm and tropic/Where Ross Perot is not the topic/All the livelong day."

So I am sitting at a table with Dora Bacoyaniss, who doubles as daughter to the Prime Minister and deputy of the ruling party, and she wants to know about Ross Perot. So does everybody else at the party and, for all I know, everybody in Macedonia.

But I am not going to do this to you, don't worry. Let me take you, instead, for drinks with Frank Sinatra.

It turns out that Athens is the last stop on his Mediterranean tour. The best thing is to catch him on the last run, it means Jack Daniels and hanging out.

The promoters booked him into a coliseum the size of Rome, and with about 20 good seats. He drew 30,000 people and sang his heart out for 100 minutes. I clocked it. A few music lovers nearby noted that he was not the same as when with Tommy Dorsey, eureka! He was terrific, fuggetaboutit.

After the show, we closed a restaurant with him and then the night itself. Near dawn, one of his people tried to get him to sleep—the plane for L.A. was leaving soon.

"What?" he said. "It's the shank of the night! Bring more bottles."

He wanted to talk about Jilly Rizzo. Jilly was killed by a drunken driver a couple of weeks ago, on his 75th birthday. As the world knows, he and Sinatra were tight for nearly 50 years. Jilly ran a great saloon on 52nd Street for a good 20 years. If you were a New Yorker and you didn't know Jilly, who the hell would do business with you. Nobody ever charged Jilly as an intellectual.

"I took him to Carnegie one Sunday for Brahms," Sinatra said. "He elbows me after a while and says, 'I've been watching this bass player closely. The bum hasn't played a fucking note in 20 minutes!'"

At intermission, somebody came over to the box. "Jilly, what are you doing here?"

"It's a *must* with me," said Jilly Rizzo.

And this is my answer if you happen to ask me how come I was drinking with Frank Sinatra and supping with the Prime Minister of Greece on a June night in Athens.

# VI

## TALES OF
## OLD PASSAIC

# THE PHANTOM AND FATHER

ꚛ ꚛ ꚛ

U ntil I was 17, I never knew anyone who paid a parking ticket. It had nothing to do with money, it was the opposite of money. A ticket was a buck, not even up to the pay-the-$2 joke. Still, mature men and women would think nothing of hanging around Julius Cinamon's junkyard for hours, waiting for him to get back from City Hall to kill the ticket.

Mr. Cinamon was the Police Commissioner of Passaic throughout most of the 40's and 50's, and for years I thought the only thing a Police Commissioner had to do was to take care of people who got parking tickets from Patty O'Keefe.

Patty was a patrolman who ran around on a motorcycle for 30 years, putting tickets on cars whose owners always swore to Julius Cinamon that they were waiting in a store for change for the meter when, "out of nowhere," Patty O'Keefe struck. He was an incorruptible cop who never got promoted, and there was a constant rumor that Julius wouldn't promote him because, as everyone knows, Julius could not just rip up the tickets; he had to pay for them himself.

So everybody figured he took it out on O'Keefe when promotion time came along.

But, of course, this was not the case. It was just what people wanted to believe, just as they would never admit that Mr. Cinamon paid for the tickets because they liked to think he killed them.

If Julius held it against Patty, he would have promoted him out of the Traffic Division. But if he did that, the public would have been up in arms, since, without Patty giving out tickets, there would have been no excuse to run over to Cinamon's junkyard to have the tickets killed.

A person who had a ticket killed by Julius Cinamon would lunch on it for weeks, and then how could he fail to vote for him without being an ingrate? It was a perfect circle that worked for 16 years.

It would have worked for 20 years, except that in 1947 a coup d'etat inside the newly elected City Commission pushed Cinamon out of the Police Department and into the Parks Department. This was remedied by the voters four years later; but in the interim, when I was 17, my father became the first person I knew to pay a parking ticket.

There is a story that goes with it, but it's time that I mentioned what brings the whole issue to the front. Earlier this month, the Superior Court in Trenton upheld a contempt citation against a teacher who paid his parking ticket, but couldn't resist sending a letter with it to the Court Clerk. The letter closed with a "vulgar obscenity," which prompted the clerk to take the letter to the magistrate, who promptly held the teacher in contempt and fined him $100.

The teacher, who probably had read somewhere that the First Amendment applied in New Jersey, appealed the case, but to little avail. The Superior Court held that the letter was "disrespectful," though not so disrespectful as to warrant more than a $25 fine.

Hard cases make bad law, as Mr. Justice Holmes taught us. Little did he know what $2 cases could do.

Until last week, I thought the Alien and Sedition Act was still dead. As far as I know, the Alien and Sedition Act was the last statute in America to punish people for making disrespectful statements about public officials. Then, again, it's the Bicentennial, so perhaps this was the court's way of bowing nostalgically to the past.

My father avoided all this trouble when he paid his first parking ticket in the winter of 1950. He sent a letter with his buck, but, having lived through the courtly era of Julius Cinamon, he showed no vulgarity whatever. And since there was no Julius to listen to the story that went with it, he told it to the Court Clerk.

"I stopped to get change of a quarter to put a nickel in the meter," my father wrote. "Mr. LoPresti, the owner of LoPresti's Luncheonette and Ice Cream Parlor, was busy, so it took a minute or two before he could change my coin. When I got outside, the ticket was there, signed by—who else?—The Phantom.

"I speak, of course, of Patrolman Patrick O'Keefe, who is never there when you're trying to spot him. But turn your head, and you have a ticket on the windshield. You can't even argue your case, because The Phantom disappears before you know he was there.

"Not that it would help if you caught him in the act, since it is well known that O'Keefe never lost an argument. I enclose my dollar for the Phantom Fund."

The clerk did not go to the court with the letter. He turned it over to a Passaic Herald-News reporter.

Instead of a constitutional confrontation, my old man was famous and Patty O'Keefe was, from that moment on, The Phantom.

I asked my dad whether, in light of the Trenton decision, he felt lucky. After all, in these parlous times there's no telling how a sensitive Court Clerk might view his letter.

"Lucky?" he replied, "If Julius had been the Police Commissioner, he'd have killed the ticket. That would have been lucky."

# AUNT GESHKA
# THE BOOTLEGGER

Y ou don't hear much of it at Sardi's bar, but in my old hangouts in Passaic people are talking about the Depression the way their fathers reminisced about the old one when I was growing up there in the 40's.

Nobody is selling apples on street corners, but the saloons are full of proud men drowning welfare checks in beer while cursing the day they went against their political heritage and voted for Nixon. "My old man told me the Republicans bring hard times," an able-bodied, unemployed factory worker said, and the bar cheered.

True or not, Gerry Ford is in trouble in Passaic, and I suspect everywhere where those who hate the dole now have to accept it to support their families.

It was an altogether melancholy weekend, listening to old pals in trouble. The saver was that it served to bring back memories of my Aunt Geshka who never said a word about hard times, even though they ran around with her for most of her long and colorful life.

"Why should I talk about it?" she told me once. "Did bad luck do so much for me that I need to be its press agent?"

She was not really my aunt, she was my Great Aunt, or my half-Great Aunt, having shared a father, but not a mother, with my grandma. And on Sundays, we called her Gussie.

Geshka had her flush times in the 20's, before I was born, and, when everybody else went broke in the Crash, she was at the top of her game, which was bootlegging. "Tevya sold milk, I sold malt," she told me years later.

It was hardly the only difference. If Geshka came out of the same herring barrel with Sholem Aleichem's dairyman, she never issued a wistful word, not to say prayer, about the rich and her God and their possible connection.

"When I never asked God for a dime, I was loaded," she said. "The minute I dunned Him, I was out of business. Whoever said the synagogue was a bull market?"

Geshka was probably the only lady bootlegger in North Jersey. As such, she could have been burned quickly, but she managed never to get busted.

"She used to load up the trunk of her Chevy with booze," my mother told me. "When she made deliveries, there was usually a priest in the front seat and a couple of nuns in the back. I remember how she'd come by my father's produce market to gas up—we had our own tanks for the trucks—in the afternoons.

"She'd introduce us to the priest and nuns, who, of course, had no idea what their role was. They'd praise her to the heavens, thinking she was such a nice lady to take them out for a drive. It was still an event to ride around in a car in those days, and they were beside themselves with gratitude. Little did they know they were working for Waxey Gordon."

Geshka was too smart to always accommodate the clergy. She'd break up the *modus operandi* by treating her youngest nieces to afternoon joy rides.

"When I couldn't have been more than 7," one of them told me the other day, "Aunt Gesh would pick me up after school and drive me around, me and my older sister. Sometimes I'd complain I'd want to go to the Jolly Juniors, which was what it sounds like, a play group.

" 'You'll go tomorrow,' Gesh would say, 'you need the air.' "

The Prohibition era was the only time Geshka ever saw real money. And she gave plenty of it away, despite the fact that she had lived through such poverty that one of her two sons died of malnutrition shortly after World War I.

Her husband divorced her in 1917 and, if there was such a thing as alimony or child support in that time, it was not for the poor immigrant. Nor was there welfare.

Geshka was the first Women's Libber I ever knew, and she dressed the part. She wore a beret, long black stockings and sneakers, and a Lucky dragged her lip in a fashion that people in Passaic to this day swear was plagiarized by Humphrey Bogart.

Few women smoked in that time, and almost none who were of uncertain age. Geshka didn't give it a thought; she was bringing up a son with no help, and she didn't think explanations were necessary.

If someone mentioned her ex-husband, who had remarried and was living in town, she'd say, "May he rest in peace." But he is not dead would come the reply. "He's dead to me," she'd say.

Geshka trusted no government, no institutions.

Still, it never occurred to her to worry about the banks. One day, F.D.R. closed them and there went her bootleg cash.

"All my life I was a one-pillow gal," she told me. "So explain to me why I didn't trust the pillow with my money?"

Geshka talked like that, the sharpest tongue in the East. That she talked English at all was a surprise to us, for we were used to hearing her contemporaries speak, at best, in a broken-Yiddish tongue. She was fluent in Polish, Spanish, Italian and, I'd bet, in Serbo-Croatian.

"It was the bootlegging days that did it," my mother says. "After all, everybody was drinking and Geshka had to talk to her customers."

When the banks closed at the same time as the Johnnie Walker ran out, Geshka had to do the best she could. My first memories of her, in the late 30's, are cluttered with canes, crutches, neck braces and eye patches. When I mentioned this recently to one of my aunts, she laughed and asked whether I recalled Geshka tossing them all off and away after spending an hour or so in our house. And I did recall it.

"Times were tough," my aunt said, "and Geshka was on her own. But there were always insurance companies and, of course, hungry negligence lawyers. Geshka knew every cracked sidewalk in Passaic, and every lawyer with a touch of larceny in him. So, whenever things got very bad, she'd have a terrible fall.

"There was no end to it, since the businessmen were broke and couldn't pay for the repairs in front of their buildings. Geshka wouldn't hurt a businessman, but the insurance companies were different. She did it so often we used to say that the lawyers kept carbons of her X-rays."

In her old age, Geshka was wracked with pain, but you'd never know it talking to her. She lived in Spanish Harlem, where all the neighbors called her momma, and when I'd go up to see her she'd talk about everything from pot to Norman Podhoretz. She was in and out of Mt. Sinai Hospital, and it was a source of pride for her that the doctors loved her and never billed her. Even so, she couldn't resist the good life.

"Why shouldn't they go for me?" she'd say. "Every day, I create new frontiers in medicine. If Geshka doesn't have it, it never happened. I've had so many operations, every time I see a knife, we make love. It's not so bad, *tatele*. At my age, you take whatever action you can get."

Geshka died at 80, or something like it, just a few years ago. I was out of town and couldn't make the funeral. But I remembered one I was at. I was, at most, 9 years old, and standing next to Aunt Geshka. The husband, whose wife had died, was threatening to jump into the grave with her, and one of my uncles was holding him back.

"Let him go," Geshka said.

"But he'll jump," my uncle said.

"Let go of him!" she said.

He let go, and the man moved toward the grave and then quickly fell backward, onto terra firma.

Geshka turned to me.

"Let that be a lesson to you," she said.

# BULLET VOTE, DUMMY!

The terrible thing about it, everyone now admits, is that I had to read it in the papers. The Mayor has the City Council President arrested for threatening his life, and nobody calls to tell me.

We are talking about my home town of Passaic, where my parents live; about Mayor Gerry Goldman, who went to school with me, and about Council President Pete Bruce, who used to buy drinks for me. But the personal connections are not so important, just as it makes no difference that I've been living in Manhattan for 10 years.

What matters is that my Cousin Maxie didn't call, which shocked my mother, who also didn't call, which outraged Sid Riskin, who also didn't call, which violated Meyer Friedman, who also didn't call. Two hundred people should have called, but nobody did, and now they all admit that something serious has happened to Passaic.

In the old days, in the 40's and 50's, my Aunt Ella would have heard about something like this—about a whole lot less than this—before *The Passaic Herald-News* knew it. My Aunt Ella lived in Miami, where she waited on tables off Biscayne Boulevard; not only would we have pulled her off duty, we did.

In May 1947, hours after the election of the Passaic Board of Commissioners, three of the five newly elected members ran off to a hideout in Connecticut. When the word broke, gloom pervaded the campaign headquarters of Julius J. Cinamon, the incumbent Police Commissioner.

Mr. Cinamon, who placed second in the voting, would nonetheless be out as the police head, since any Big Three that could be put together would have the power to strip the other two. Police was the best department, and it was obvious at the Cinamon headquarters that the new crowd was going to take him down and put him somewhere like Parks, which is what they did.

But they could not have reached the Merritt Parkway before my cousin Hank had Aunt Ella on the phone. Ella was so upset by the news that my Uncle Jake had to talk her out of coming back to demand a recall.

It was not that Ella was some kind of political powerhouse; it was simply that everyone who once lived in Passaic considered themselves eternal citizens of Passaic, and those who stayed behind thought the same.

On Election Day, the town was full of people who had moved as far away as Miami and as close by as Paterson. They would vote here, they weren't fooling around, they weren't here just for the color.

As far as I could tell, nobody challenged them, although everybody knew they had moved. It was all considered honest because none of them had voted in their new home cities. Why vote elsewhere when you could vote for Commissioners in Passaic?

I've covered national political conventions since leaving home, but nothing ever came close to a Passaic election, including Chicago, 1968. Then, as now, it was nonpartisan; then, as now, it was hotly ethnic.

We called it a Beauty Contest among Italians, Jews and Poles. The League of Women Voters and other good citizens' groups were forever dismayed, the campaigns being entirely devoid of issues, but it was lively doings and, for a kid with a car, it was a nice day's pay.

The first election I worked was in 1951, it being the first one I had a driver's license to show. Looking back, it was the last great one we had in town, and the first ever in which two Jews were likely to win. I drove for both of them—Julius Cinamon and Morris Pashman, now on the New Jersey Supreme Court—and, to prove my ecumenism, for Ben Manney, who was Italian.

All three won, and I picked up 75 bucks, plus gas. Mainly, we'd go around picking up old people, and it didn't hurt Ben at all that both his names sounded Jewish. I even tricked my grandma into voting for him, which was no easy deal after what happened in 1947.

Before the '47 election, my grandma, like many old-timers of all persuasions, was given to "bullet voting," a tactic publicly disdained by all but indulged in plenty. You were supposed to vote for five Commissioners, but nobody could make you do it.

A bullet was a vote for one only, and for years grandma went that route for Julius Cinamon, who lived next door to us. Julius had lost in his first outing, in 1935, by fewer than 50 votes, and the Jews decided never to let that happen again. So my grandmother, who would say she was voting for five, and even seven, would not vote until the last minute.

"I want to wait for the rumors," she'd tell me. The rumors always came, generally through Julius's mother, who'd come to our porch at 6 P.M. and tell grandma that the Poles were wiping out Jules on the East Side and the fancy gentiles were cutting him uptown.

As it turned out, Julius did terrific everywhere, but my grandma—and who knows how many more?—took care of him alone. "Don't ask questions," she'd say to me after I walked her over to the polls, and when we got home, she'd give the wink to Mrs. Cinamon.

In 1947, her enlightened grandchildren convinced her to vote a full ticket, which included two Poles and two Italians. So it turned out that the Poles bulleted "theirs," and Julius was stuck with the Parks Department. Never again, said grandma, and she went to her grave believing that Ben Manney was a Jew.

In the middle 60's, after I had left town, the Good Government people finally succeeded in changing the form of government, not once but twice. Passaic now has a strong Mayor-Council system, which looks terrific on paper, no doubt about it.

The difference is that few people seem to care anymore; the Mayor gets fewer votes now than the sixth, seventh and eighth also-rans garnered in the past. The population has dropped, to be sure, but not nearly by that much. And nobody shows up from out of town on Election Day.

Blame it on crime, on the economy, on inertia. When the Mayor arrests the President of the City Council and I have to read it in the papers, I know, and now my people know, that Trouble has come to River City. Was it John O'Hara who said that an era is over when the laughs are gone?

# RUTGERS VS. THE WONDER TEAM, 1920'S

The Rutgers basketball team is said to have made everyone in New Jersey forget his troubles, but pardon us old Passaicites if we yawn a little. The 26 regular-season games won by the Scarlet Knights isn't bad for what it is, but what is it next to the 159 consecutive victories rolled up by the Passaic High School Indians of the early 20's?

The Wonder Team, they called it all over the country, and no wonder. In the history of competitive sports in America, nothing has ever approached this record. It put my town on the map, and kept it there for so long that the first thing my father-in-law-to-be said to me when we met in the early 60's was, "Wow! Passaic! That's the Wonder Five, that was the greatest basketball team ever put together."

And my father-in-law is from Winthrop, N.Y., which, in case you never heard of it, is a sneeze and a quarter from the Canadian border.

It didn't surprise me, not even slightly. Every-where I traveled, as soon as I said I was from Passaic, somebody would say something about the Wonder Team; and, of course, the same thing happened to my friends, all of whom, like me, were born a decade or so after the streak was broken. It made no difference that we weren't around to see the team, it was part of the fabric of the city.

Johnny Roosma, who went on to West Point and the basketball Hall of Fame; Bobby Thompson, whose real name was Thousand-Point Bobby Thompson; Ira Vonk, Fritz Knothe, Paul Blood—all of them and many more were as real to us as Joe DiMaggio.

Not only would we hear about them from our parents, they'd also turn up at Father-and-Son luncheons (do they still have Father-and-Son luncheons?), or at high-school graduations or at half-time at the semipro basketball games (they do not still have semipro basketball games).

One time after World War II, a few of the Wonder Five got back into uniform for an Old-Timers game at Kanter's Auditorium, and when DeWitt Kiesler sank a 20-footer, it was the second time I saw grown men cry. The first time was at an All-Star game at Yankee Stadium in 1944, when tears streamed down my Uncle Mac's cheeks after Babe Ruth put one into the right-field seats.

But enough sentiment. When *The New York Times* proclaimed on Page 1 the happiness of New Jerseyans over Rutgers, the first thing I did was to call Milton Pashman.

Milton Pashman is a lawyer, and he is also the Deputy Surrogate of Passaic County. And even if he were Governor, he still would be known as "Milton Pashman, the Captain of the Last Wonder Team."

On Feb. 6, 1925—Black Friday—at the Hackensack Armory, the Hackensack High School basketball team beat Passaic, 39–35.

"I felt like it was the end of the world," Mr. Pashman said the other day from his Paterson office. "I scored 17 points that day, but I was the captain and I blamed myself. It was a horror. The whole town closed down, Passaic went into mourning. Businesses actually closed, for nobody had the heart to make money that day. An era was over."

In any event, the 1925 Indians went on to win the state championship and, better yet, the nationwide interscholastic title at a tournament held in Glens Falls, N.Y.

"Hackensack," Mr. Pashman said, "was upset by Plainfield in an early round of the state championship. We then killed Plainfield. In all, I think we won 15 or 16 games straight after losing to Hackensack, so we'd have had about 175 straight if we could have scored another five points on Feb. 6. I'll never forget the date.

"But Hackensack was the better team. After the tournament was over in Glens Falls, we played them in what was styled as an exhibition game and they beat us again, 37–26."

I asked Mr. Pashman whether his career was hurt by the breaking of the skein.

"What do you mean?" he laughed. "I've been a loser ever since. Every time I ran for office, I was defeated. How could you explain that otherwise? A man with my talent and personality, I could have been Governor, I could have been Senator."

Then he added, "kidding aside," that it had made him famous, that terrible day in Hackensack.

"The only captains they all remember are me and Johnny Roosma," Mr. Pashman said. "When I'm on the dais with Johnny, I always say, 'Well there's the guy who started it and here's the guy who ended it.'"

Basketball was so different in those days that it

almost seems like another game from today. For example, there was a center jump after every basket, which gave teams with tall centers a terrific edge. And each team could designate one man to shoot all fouls.

"Paul Blood shot all our fouls," Mr. Pashman went on. "He just about never missed. He was the son of Prof. Ernest Blood, who coached the Wonder Team all the way through. It was a very fast game we played. Don't kid yourself by some of the low scores.

"Blood was a great coach and we were very disciplined. It was a passing game mainly, with the emphasis on getting the ball to the open man for a layup.

"And only near the end were the scores so low. I played in at least four games where we scored over 100 points. In the first couple of years of the streak, this happened all the time. We had big guys, you know. Ira Vonk, the center, was maybe 6-10. So we didn't lose that center jump too often."

Last year, the Wonder Team was installed into the basketball Hall of Fame, on the occasion of the 50th anniversary of the streak's demise.

"It's nice to know people don't forget," Milton Pashman said.

"How long will they remember Rutgers?" I asked him.

"How much is 26 from 159?" he replied.

# VII

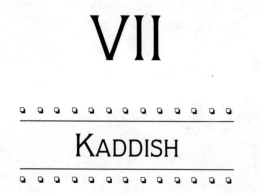

## KADDISH

# BILL DOUGLAS

There is a dream and a reality in America, and though they lie on the same bed they are never expected to kiss. The dream is Jimmy Stewart out of Frank Capra, and it says, Be True to Yourself. The reality is Sam Rayburn out of the World of Men, and it says, To Get Along, Go Along. As children we are instructed in the dream, as adults in the reality. We are never taught to forget the dream, but are asked instead to ignore the contradiction. The end becomes a Rhinestone Mean: To get along with the dream, go along with the reality.

Bill Douglas treated the reality as dirt under his feet, and rode the dream straight to the top. That this made him a unique phenomenon is one of the more melancholy facts of the twentieth century. Surely nothing would have astonished and enraged the Framers more than that there was only one Bill Douglas—unless it is that there will probably never be another.

"I am really a pretty conservative fellow from the old school," he said when F.D.R. appointed him to the Court. The line was widely resurrected as irony when the stroke forced him to quit in 1975, after a record-breaking thirty-six years on the High Bench. Had he not, it was pointedly asked, become the most flamboyant liberal ever to sit there? It wasn't Douglas who changed, but the meaning of words, which was distorted just as the Bill of Rights is today distorted by the Burger Court. The true meaning of conservative, the first dictionary definition, is a synonym for preservative. To conserve, to preserve, is to "keep from injury or destruction; defend from evil; protect; save." What better way to describe William O. Douglas's glorious career on the Supreme Court than that it was fiercely dedicated—against all the winds that blew—to the conservation, the preservation, of the Constitution?

A conservative fellow from the old school. Philadelphia, class of 1776. Can't you just see Bill there, trading ideas, swapping stories, passing the flask with Jefferson, Madison, Franklin, Sam Adams? Now picture Warren Burger, William Rehnquist and the rest of that passel of statists who made up the "conservative" majority on the Court. Is there anyone out there who thinks they would have been allowed past the rope?

Other modern-day Justices would have been more or less at home in Philadelphia—Louis Brandeis, Hugo Black, Earl Warren, William Brennan, Frank Murphy, Wiley Rutledge, Harlan Stone, John Harlan, maybe another handful. But Bill would have fit best. He could sit a horse, fish a stream, climb a mountain with any of the frontiersmen. And looked the part—perhaps more as he aged, when the weathered, ruggedly lined face added rather to the impression of strength than years.

Douglas looked so much like his pal Spencer Tracy that he was often mistaken for him; later, Casey Stengel was mistaken for *him*. He was a lanky six-footer, with direct, blue-gray eyes that seemed always to be taking the measure of pose and pretense; in other words, a straightaway guy you could trust but better not cross.

The Founders would have been comfortable with his language: salty, to-the-jugular, often profane. Most important, they'd have loved his elegantly blunt definition of the Great Charter: "The Constitution was designed to take the government off the backs of the people." Yet it was over that truism that the great legal war was fought during Douglas's time on the Court.

He won many battles, but at his death the result was in doubt, to say the least. Liberties thought by the Framers to have been immutably writ in the Bill of Rights are now in the hands of men who appear to believe that the essential purpose of the Supreme Court is to keep the people off the back of the government.

"His life, like his law, is free," Yale law professor Fred Rodell wrote of Douglas. For both reasons he was often under siege. Once in the 1950's, while Douglas was fighting Harry Truman's cold war (off the Court) and McCarthyism (on the Court), the great populist, Senator William Langer, put his arm around Bill and said: "Douglas, they have thrown several buckets of shit over you. But by God, none of it stuck. And I am proud." They tried three times to impeach him: in 1953, when he stayed the execution of the Rosenbergs; in 1966, when he married 23-year-old Cathleen Heffernan, now his widow, and in 1970. The last was the most serious, because it followed Abe Fortas's forced resignation from the Court and was thus part of the Nixon Gang's furious effort to deal a quick deathblow to civil liberties. Gerald Ford, the House minority leader, led the egregious attack . . . and again, none of it stuck.

The academics continued to deny him the pantheon. In 1972, the Association of American Law Schools polled sixty-five people: law school deans, law professors and professors of history and political science.

Asked to name the Hall of Fame of the Supreme Court, the professors came up with twelve stalwarts. Douglas wasn't even close. Nor would he be close today. The rap is that he was "result-oriented." A dozen years ago, I asked Douglas about it. His answer: "At the beginning of every term, I offer to bet the Brethren that I can call their votes on 98 percent of the cases. I get no takers. Once you're here for a while it's easy to predict how you'll go, the issues aren't that different. The academics call it 'result-oriented' when they don't like the result. Otherwise it's 'scholarship' "

In the event, they compliment him by their contempt. "I had my own dreams," he once wrote, "and they were dependent solely on me, not on the whim or caprice of another." They tell me he's gone now. Well, as John O'Hara said when Gershwin got away, I don't have to believe it if I don't want to.

□□□
# FRED RODELL
□□□

I n the wee small hours at Toots Shor's long ago, I saw
Frank Sinatra kiss Joe E. Lewis good night, just as the
great comic dragged himself off for a little shut-eye
before the morning bottle. Wistfully, Sinatra said to
nobody in particular: "Every time I say good night to
that lovely sonofabitch I gotta figure on saying good-
bye." Fred Rodell, the fabulous iconoclast of the Yale
Law School, who died on June 4 at the age of 73, never
let me forget that incident. For the past decade, Rodell
was beset with a plague of Jobian illnesses. Every time I
talked to him, I had to figure it was the last time. Like
Joe E., he kept fooling the medics; unlike Job, he didn't
cry out to the heavens. His only complaints were that
his drinking days were done and that he didn't have the
strength to discomfit his enemies.

Long before the Man in the Bright Nightgown
came to call, many of Rodell's foes had cashed in—
most notably Felix Frankfurter, Dean Acheson, Alexander Bickel. Fred took no pleasure in these funerals;
indeed, it galled him to lose such fancy targets, no
matter that his typewriter was fast running out of
bullets. Rodell knew that other typewriters were working and that he had trained most of them. He also knew

that however dead the enemies, the Enemy would live on, for it is an old one, as old as the human soul.

Fred Rodell's enemies were powerful ones, upright and uptight. The Enemy was fear posing as responsibility, pedantry dressed like scholarship, cant parading as truth. He devoted his extraordinary talents to fighting them and it, while at the same time extolling his Charter, which turned out to be no more or less than the Bill of Rights.

He said it in everything he wrote and did, but I think he said it best in the old *American Mercury* in 1945: "Two paths in life are open to the college bright boy. One is to devote that first-rate mind relentlessly to the discovery and expression of naked truth, no matter whose toes may be trampled or whose sacred cow gored. The other is to shade intellectual integrity and courage to get on well in the world—to confine that mind and the work of that mind within the bounds of acceptability to the right people, the best people, the powers that be."

Of course, Rodell followed the first path, and though he altogether eschewed the second, he was acceptable, for a glorious moment, to some of the powers that be. The Warren Court, or at least its majority, greatly respected him. In my days at *The New York Times*, more than one Justice told me that Rodell knew more about them, was better able to analyze and predict them, than all the fancy scholars rolled into one. And at his home in Bethany, Connecticut, next to a picture of Hugo Black and a bust of Bill Douglas, hangs the photograph of the 1968 Supreme Court, featuring this message: "To Fred Rodell, than whom this court has had no greater friend, from his friend Earl Warren."

In a way he lived too long; he didn't need to see the Burger Court undermine nearly everything the Warren Court had accomplished. Still, his *Nine Men,* written in 1955, was a precursor to *The Brethren,* and eons better and wiser than that current best seller. And he was more than a little pleased to be around when Berkley Publishing this year reprinted his 1939 opus, *Woe Unto You, Lawyers!* to rave reviews, particularly from young people who were surprised to see that somebody knew all about legal gobbledygook forty years ago.

Rodell's greatest influence lay in the unique seminar he taught at Yale called "Law and Public Opinion." It was a course devoted to teaching lawyers to write about the law in the English language. It spawned, like Jolson, Crosby and Sinatra, hundreds of imitators. And in journalism it turned out the first generation of lawyer-journalists.

But I don't want to miss the man in all this. What Fred Rodell had, the thing about him, was his attractiveness; a romantic allure that only the dullest could not see. For those of us fortunate enough to be there in the 1950's, the Yale Law School was, above all, Fred Rodell. He was the one who had been everywhere, seen everything. They knew him at Sardi's and at Frankie and Johnnie's and at the Ritz in Paris. He was our Bogart, to be found (why not?) in all the gin joints in all the towns in all the world.

The last words he said to me were these: "I'll see you in hell." I'll check it out, and if he's there, I'm coming.

# DANCING IN THE DARK

QQQ

Howard Dietz could iron the ironies with anybody on the block, but it's hard to believe he'd believe a eulogy in *Rolling Stone*. The music promoted by this paper never had anything good to say to Dietz, and vice versa. But rock did shut him out of the marketplace, which is why I'm going to have to do some explaining about Howard Who? that would have gone without saying had either Dietz or rock & roll died twenty-five years ago.

This is a very large statement, but I make it without hesitation: Howard Dietz ranks with the greatest lyricists in history. That is to say, with Lorenz Hart, Cole Porter, Johnny Mercer, Ira Gershwin, Irving Berlin, Frank Loesser, Yip Harburg, Alan Jay Lerner and Oscar Hammerstein II. In this pantheon, Dietz was the least well known, probably because he didn't like to publicize himself, an irony in itself since throughout his glorious career as a songwriter, he doubled as publicity chief for Metro-Goldwyn-Mayer. But the world sang his words, and a survey of just a few of his titles should make the point. So: "Dancing in the Dark," "I Guess I'll Have to Change My Plan," "You and the Night and the Music," "Alone Together," "That's Entertainment," "Something to Remember You By," "By Myself," "If There Is Someone Lovelier Than You."

These standards, plus a gang of others—nearly all of them written with Arthur Schwartz—provided Dietz more than enough filthy lucre to keep several families, with maybe a couple of great aunts thrown in. So it always intrigued me that he kept his job at MGM. I always figured songwriters thought that no matter how tough it was, it beat working, and I never heard of any of them going to somebody else's office every day. Johnny Mercer used to tell a story about his wife, Ginger, dancing with a Japanese gentleman on a crossing to merry old England. The man asked what her husband did, and she said he was a songwriter. And the guy said, "Yes, but what does he do for a *living*?"

It turns out that Howard Dietz believed that, too, and lived it out. After he died, I called Arthur Schwartz and asked him why Dietz kept his job. Schwartz said, "He wanted the security."

Actually, he was far more than a publicity man for MGM. In a town known as much for the knife in the back as the back slap, Howard Dietz was, by all accounts, one of a kind: straightforward, honorable, generous. As a result, he became a confidant to the biggest stars in Tinseltown. "They trusted him; they trusted his judgment," said Schwartz. "He'd often act as a kind of go-between. He'd talk to the stars and straighten out things with the bosses. I'm not sure those large egos loved it that the stars thought so much of Howard, but they benefited by it, so they kept their mouths shut."

Fortunately for the studio, Dietz didn't keep his mouth shut at a critical moment. During the TV scare of the late 40's, when Hollywood thought it was finished, the geniuses at MGM were on the verge of selling the studio's entire library of movies to TV for $38 million. Dietz went to the top and convinced them that *Gone with the Wind* alone was worth ten times that figure.

Dietz probably would have been worth considerably more money had he chucked the movie job. "We lost countless film assignments because Howard couldn't squeeze in the time," says Arthur Schwartz. "As it was, we always worked at strange hours, on trains, in hotel rooms, on the move all the time. Of course, Howard cheated on the workday at the studio from time to time. Once, Louis Mayer said to him, 'You always come in late.' And Howard said, 'But I leave early.'"

He was a wonderful raconteur, possessed of a sparkling wit. You could see it in his autobiography, *Dancing in the Dark*. Which on the flap cover has this: "What is this tome/And I reply/An ography/That's autobi." Plus, my favorite lead: "Nothing memorable happened until I was seven, when I stole the month's wages of Lizzie Kutchardy, our Hungarian housemaid."

The trouble is you can't buy the book. Published in 1974 to rave reviews, it was removed from the stands by Quadrangle, *The New York Times'* book company, because a lawyer threatened a libel suit over something Howard said about her. I was told the *Times* ended up burning all the books, believe it or not, and I hate to believe it.

I didn't get to meet Dietz until a couple of years ago, when he was badly debilitated by Parkinson's disease and a fall that left him unable to get around. Frankie MacCormick of the Songwriter's Hall of Fame—of course, Dietz is in it—arranged a birthday

party for him and somehow got Tiny Tim to sing.
Howard enjoyed it as best he could, but he didn't look
too good, and I wondered what that face must have
been like in his salad days. Well, old Frankie MacC
came through again; she sent me the book, and there
he was as a sailor in World War I, looking like a mid-
dleweight champ, busted nose and all.

I mentioned this to Arthur Schwartz. I said, "Howard sure didn't look like he wrote. I mean, he wrote
something like a straight Noël Coward, but he looked
like a rough guy, a pug." Schwartz laughed. "Somebody
broke the nose, and he never fixed it, but he wasn't a
tough guy—he was the gentlest, loveliest man I ever
knew."

From his book you can see why he didn't repair
the schnoz. Here's a touch of a poem he wrote called
"School Days."

> *At public school*
> *I made no sense*
> *But learned the art*
> *Of self-defense*
> *From kindergarten*
> *to 6B*
> *I went to P.S.*
> *103*
> *And what with all*
> *The cons and pros*
> *I left there*
> *With a broken nose*

He was born in 1896, so much a child of this
century. He must have loved children, or why would he
have done the following for young Jonathan Schwartz,

Arthur's son, later to become a top disc jockey. In 1953, Schwartz and Dietz turned their hit show *The Band Wagon* into a movie. Dietz arranged the city-by-city premieres to coincide with the Boston Red Sox' schedule, just to please Jonathan, who was one of the world's foremost Red Sox freaks.

"The film opened in Boston," Jonathan told me, "and went where the Red Sox went—Detroit, Cleveland, Chicago. Cyd Charisse was the star, and one day I took Howard up on a long-standing bet. He bet me he could write a lyric about anything in ten seconds. So I said, 'Cyd Charisse.' And without blinking he said, 'Cyd Charisse/Get off the mantelpiece/You're quite a shock there/We need a clock there.'"

It amounts to this. A Jewish kid named Dietz, who looks like a Polish fighter, hooks up with a Jewish lawyer named Schwartz, and instead of making dresses, they make songs. And such songs! The first time you heard them, you knew nothing would be the same again.

"You want to sum up his thinking in a couple of lines?" asked Arthur Schwartz.

> We're waltzing in the wonder
> Of why we're here
> Time hurries by—we're here
> And gone

"Howard wrote it," said Arthur Schwartz "and Howard was right."

# ALDEN WHITMAN

In his fifty-second year on this wicked old planet, Alden Whitman concluded that there was one too many lines in Ecclesiastes. And just like that, he knew he could create something new under the sun. With *The New York Times* as his calling card, he'd travel the world interviewing its movers and shakers, promising them one thing only: They would never get to read what he wrote about them.

In all the history of journalism, including the caves, nobody ever thought to draw the future dead into their own obituaries, and if anybody had he would surely not have had the chutzpah to condition the deal on never seeing the product. "All is vanity, a striving after wind," says Ecclesiastes, and Alden knew better than to discard that wisdom. If they had the vanity he'd give 'em all the wind they wanted. He turned obits into an art form, he put the death page on Page One, and he gave us history on the hoof.

In the doing, he turned himself into the most sought-after reporter on the *Times,* which is to say in the world. After Alden Whitman there was no second act. Ho Chi Minh knew that, as did Pablo Picasso, Harry Truman, Francis Cardinal Spellman, Charlie

Chaplin, Earl Warren, Henry Miller, Albert Schweitzer, Charles Lindberg, Henry Luce, Maurice Chevalier, Joseph Kennedy, Helen Keller, Haile Selassie, Harry Bridges, Norman Thomas, Mies van der Rohe and Israel Schawarzberg.

All of the above lent themselves willingly to the Alden Whitman treatment, but none put it better than Israel Schawarzberg, who was not a Russian violinist or a Budapest conductor—forget about it. Izzy was the last great single-o act in the American-Jewish underworld, and so attracted the sharp eye of Whitman, who spent several nights with him a couple of months before Izzy met his Maker.

Schawarzberg was only 56 at the time and apparently in good health. But as soon as he concluded his interviews with Alden, he said to me, "When I go, I want you to call Alden Whitman first. Forget about my wife, forget about my brothers, forget about my father. Just remember to call Whitman. I want an Alden Whitman obit, otherwise no good!"

I was lunching with Alden at Sardi's when the call came that Izzy was gone. Izzy got the full treatment, across the top of the page, picture with it, and to hell with whoever else went that day, including a Big Steel executive. It was a terrific piece and it made the network news that night. Twenty years later, the day Alden Whitman died, I mentioned this incident to Arthur Gelb, who was the metropolitan editor of the *Times* during Whitman's flush years on the paper.

"He had uncanny timing," Gelb said. "When Alden Whitman did you, you died. It happened all the time. It was amazing. You might be larky, feeling younger than springtime, a glass of champagne in your hand, that night you made love to your wife. But after Alden Whitman came to call, you were history."

And now, as it must to all men ... Alden Whitman.

I have done him short justice here, leaving out even the highlights: That he was a man of the left and a contributor to *The Nation*. That he refused to name names when the Senate went after him for his membership in the Communist Party and that he worked his way out of the cold storage the *Times* had put him in.

That he refused to give up when the wheelchair and blindness got him. That in the end, as in the beginning, he was a newspaperman. And that as such, he was subject to the only rule he could not change. As wrote Ben Hecht of a departed colleague on the Chicago *Journal* in 1920:

*We know each other's daydreams*
*And the hopes that come to grief*
*For we write each other's obits*
*And they're Godalmighty brief.*

ㅁㅁㅁ

# A GIRL NAMED LIBBY

ㅁㅁㅁ

The editorial in the Journal of the American Medical Association put it this way: "Libby Zion's death has changed residency training forever. The public is outraged that life-and-death decisions are made by residents working 36-hour shifts and 100-hour weeks ... There is no turning back."

When there appeared to be no question that "forever" was safely berthed in New York, state regulations were established requiring the presence of experienced doctors in the emergency room at all times. State regulations limiting residents to no more than 24 hours of work in a shift and 80 hours in a week were to take effect July 1.

Our family took solace. Libby had not died in vain. She was 18 on that Sunday night nine years ago when we walked her into the emergency room at New York Hospital with an earache and fever. In the morning, they sent her back to us in a box, another victim of a system whose rationale—"It's good for the doctors to work so hard"—guaranteed disaster for untold numbers of patients.

But Libby Zion was not just another victim. They had killed the "wrong kid," whose father, with his access to the media and politicians, refused to be a good sport, wouldn't accept a "sorry" and a check.

I wanted indictments and I wanted the system revamped. I didn't get indictments, but in January 1987 a Manhattan grand jury, blasting the hospital for its "woefully inadequate" care of Libby, made broad recommendations for reform. This led Dr. David Axelrod, the State Health Commissioner, to convene a blue-ribbon commission, which led to the regulations.

In April of 1989, *The New York Times* reported a "raging debate" had suddenly emerged over the limitation of hours. Who starts a debate after the deal is done? And what's debatable? You don't need kindergarten to know that a resident working a 36-hour shift is in no condition to make any kind of judgment call—forget about life-and-death. This debate had already been fought out by the commission. But the hospital doctors' lobby is relentless, as my family well knows.

In response to the grand jury report, New York Hospital put out a news release charging that Libby died of a cocaine overdose. This was a complete fabrication, discredited by all medical and scientific authorities, including the top brass at New York Hospital itself.

When you blame the victim, the real victim is truth. But what appeal has truth to those intent upon maintaining the status quo?

So the "raging debate" turned into a lobbying effort in the Legislature during last month's budget jockeying. We can't afford it, said the hospitals. They'd been running a slave-labor system for a hundred years, how could they pay for more residents?

But Dr. Axelrod and Gov. Mario Cuomo had allocated $270 million for the reforms in the current budget. The hospitals said, we need the money for more "primary" purposes; reallocate the dollars. The Legislature refused. The hospitals answered: "We can't find enough residents. What good is the money?"

It's not money, it's not bodies and it never has been. Fundamentally, it's sovereignty. Doctor Knows Best. To change the system now is to say they've been wrong. For a century! Try and tell the average doc he was wrong for five minutes and you know what I mean.

If Dr. Axelrod didn't know, he knows now. The New York State Medical Society demanded his resignation for issuing "oppressive, arbitrary and unnecessarily burdensome" regulations. Then the Hospital Association of New York State brought suit to enjoin him from implementing the new rules on resident hours.

Not that they're against the reforms, God forbid. It's just not the propitious time, too many other things on the table, we've got to take care of the patients.

But if this time goes by, the patient will never be in the equation. On the other hand, if we wake up, make our voices heard, one day they'll teach in medical schools around the world: "Once upon a time in America, the finest hospitals were run by the least experienced and most overworked apprentice doctors. Until one Sunday night in New York, a red-headed girl named Libby Zion . . ."

# HOSPITALS CAN BE DEADLY

Y ankel Rosenbaum came up from Australia to study the Holocaust and commune with his Rebbe in Brooklyn, and he was killed twice. First by a lynch mob who left him for dead in the streets, and then at the hands of inexperienced and unsupervised residents in a hospital emergency room.

If the knives fail, there are always the doctors.

We are left to wonder what images ran through his mind as he lay bleeding to death in the place he was taken to be saved. It could not have been Dr. Mengele, for nobody meant to harm him at Kings County Hospital. He was dead because he was a Jew. What finally killed him was the evil of banality.

Yankel Rosenbaum would have survived if the authorities at Kings County Hospital had followed State Health Department regulations requiring supervision of inexperienced residents. Those regulations were officially promulgated in July 1989 and are commonly known as the *Libby Zion Regulations*, after my daughter, who died in 1984 at the hands of inexperienced and unsupervised interns and residents at New York Hospital.

The regulations included the cutting of dangerously long, slave labor hours for interns and residents. They were fought against viciously by the doctors' lobby, who seemed to think that their lives, not ours, were at stake. But through the tenacity of David Axelrod, then the State Health Commissioner, and Dr. Bertram Bell, who headed the commission to study the situation in the wake of Libby's death, the reforms were achieved. And they were hailed by the media and the public, and they have set about reform movements in several states and even continents.

To my family it meant that Libby had not died in vain. The promise to the people of New York was that hospitals would no longer be killing fields—for of course, no regulations would have been mandated based on the death of one 18-year-old girl. This condition was found to be widespread, "systemic," in the words of a New York County grand jury report on Libby's death that laid the groundwork for the regulations.

So Yankel Rosenbaum was supposed to have been saved by the death of Libby Zion. And Yankel Rosenbaum is dead because the powers that be at Kings County did not think it necessary to have competent doctors running the emergency room. We know now that one of the two female residents who were left in charge of Mr. Rosenbaum's case had been previously dismissed from another surgical training program. But egregious as this is—and egregious as was the failure of this third-year resident to detect a fatal stab wound in Yankel Rosenbaum's chest, even though she was told about it by the ambulance crew—it is important that we not view the event as anecdotal.

For what happened to Yankel Rosenbaum could still happen in most hospitals in New York and probably is happening as we speak. Indeed, the horror of Harlem Hospital, where overcrowding recently led a resident to turn away a woman about to give birth, is an example of the flaunting of the regulation requiring supervision by fully qualified doctors. "Get out of my face," this resident reportedly said to the husband of the pregnant woman, and that might be the metaphor for the attitude of our great healers. If we're smart, it will be the shot across the bow of our complacency, or rather our brainwashed minds. We have revered the medics and so turned them into a priesthood above the law.

Even as I write this, I know it is not true. People on the streets, in the saloons and in the finest salons understand full well that something terrible is going on in the medical profession and in our hospitals. Only they don't think they can do anything about it, and who can blame them?

The public is always frustrated, at wit's end, when the media are silent and the politicians are at rest or busy with other things. The press always listens to the loudest voices, and those voices inevitably belong to the politicians. Alas, the pols have seldom had the stomach to take on the American Medical Association.

It does not mean it has to be this way. Of course not. The doctors' lobby was cracked by Libby's death, and it can be packed away by the death of Yankel Rosenbaum. If we do it right.

The first thing to do is call in the cops. The criminal negligence statutes do not insulate the medical profession. These laws, which govern cases of drunken or reckless driving and all sorts of events in which nobody meant to do it, do not require malicious intent for a prosecution to succeed. A few years ago, a construction crane on the East Side of Manhattan went down and crushed the legs of a female pedestrian. The police were there in a trice, and hours later everybody was printed and booked—the foreman, the safety supervisor and the guy who did the deed. And they were all indicted.

They didn't mean to do it, but they had been guilty of criminal negligence. The supervisor had failed to supervise properly, the foreman put an inexperienced man on the crane and the man on the crane shouldn't have undertaken the responsibility.

The only difference between that event and what happened to Libby—and what happened to Yankel Rosenbaum—was that the culprits in one case wore hard hats and in the other case white coats.

But that is some difference. Not in law but in practice. In practice, the white coats have defacto immunity from prosecution for criminal negligence.

I think Robert Morgenthau was the first District Attorney in the country to convene a grand jury on the issue of medical malpractice. It was in Libby's case, and I remember telling him that story about the construction gang, hoping he'd indict the doctors. He didn't indict, but he did produce a grand jury report that led to the regulations we have been talking about.

Still, I thought then, and I know now, that such compromise with the law will not suffice to protect the public against white coat crimes.

Hospitals can be dangerous to our health. They will not become fully safe because the Health Department issues regulations, and Health Department inspectors do the investigations, and doctor-ruled disciplinary committees decide who shall practice and who shall not.

It was only because City Council President Andrew J. Stein demanded an investigation of Kings County Hospital that we know what happened to Yankel Rosenbaum. (So much for those, like Mayor Dinkins, who say Mr. Stein's office is irrelevant and should be abolished.) And of course it was only because I had friends in the media and in the government that we were able to make Libby's death more than an anecdote in the dustbins of medical malpractice.

But it ought not require friends in high places or media events to actuate law enforcement. It should be automatic.

Charles J. (Joe) Hynes, the District Attorney of Brooklyn, has begun an investigation of the Yankel Rosenbaum death. Mr. Hynes cut his teeth as counsel to Andy Stein in the nursing home hearings 15 years ago. He is hip to crimes that happen under white coats.

I said to Joe Hynes the other day that the first D.A. who opens a medical malpractice bureau will make history. Just one person to start, and in a year it will be larger than the rackets squad.

Hey, more people die by doctors every year than by AIDS, and there's a Congressional study that proves it. I wrote about that in this newspaper in 1987. You can look it up.

# Publisher's Note

The majority of the pieces in this book appeared in *The New York Observer*, 1991–1993. The others:

Growing Up With the Mob—*The New York Times*, January 11, 1976

Champ Segal—*The New York Post*, October 25, 1977

Israel Schawarzberg—*The New York Post*, December 20, 1977

Who's Crazy Now?—*The New York Post*, December 1, 1977

The Cigar Crisis—*Penthouse*, April, 1993

Feeling Runyonesque—*The National Review*, June 8, 1992

While England Sleeps—*Penthouse*, July, 1990

The Conspiracy Theory—*The New York Times*, March 2, 1969

The Phantom and Father—*The New York Times*, February 15, 1976

Aunt Geshka the Bootlegger—*The New York Times*, February 8, 1976

The Hiss Case—*New York Magazine*, April 24, 1978

Alger Hiss, Esq.—*The Soho Weekly News*, August 14, 1975

Call It Sleep—*The New York Times*, January 4, 1988

Sabra, Shatila & Iraq—*The New York Daily News*,
   April 4, 1991

Bullet Vote, Dummy!—*The New York Times*,
   January 18, 1976

Rutgers vs. The Wonder Team, 1920's—*The New
   York Times*, March 7, 1976

Bill Douglas—*The Nation*, February 2, 1980

Fred Rodell—*The Nation*, June 21, 1980

Dancing in the Dark—*Rolling Stone*, September 15,
   1983

Alden Whitman—*The Nation*, October 1, 1990

A Girl Named Libby—*The New York Times*, May
   13, 1989

# INDEX